BIBLE TRUTHS

for a

LIFE OF PURPOSE

ED CYZEWSKI

BARBOUR BOOKS
An Imprint of Barbour Publishing, Inc.

Published by Barbour Books, an imprint of Barbour Publishing, Inc., 1810 Barbour Drive, Uhrichsville, Ohio 44683, www.barbourbooks.com

Our mission is to inspire the world with the life-changing message of the Bible.

Member of the
Evangelical Christian
Publishers Association

Printed in the United States of America.

CONTENTS

INTRODUCTION

This book, *101 Bible Truths for a Life of Purpose*, features devotional readings reflecting on Bible truths and promises for consideration, meditation, and application. It's our prayer that they will sink deep down into your heart and help you discover the secret to a fulfilling, abundant life—a life of purpose in Christ.

Many Christians desire to learn how to apply scriptures to their pressing needs, and it's perfectly legitimate to want to know how to "ask God for things." Jesus did, after all, command His disciples to pray, "Give us this day our daily bread" (Matthew 6:11). But you must have things in perspective. Matthew 6:33 says, "Seek ye first the kingdom of God, and his righteousness; and all these things shall be added unto you."

Remember also 2 Peter 1:4, which says, "Whereby are given unto us exceeding great and precious promises: that by these ye might be partakers of the divine nature." Many of God's "great and precious promises" are designed to meet your physical needs, but more than anything, He longs to transform you into the image of Christ through them. He wants to unite you spiritually with Himself so that you can partake of His divine nature, His love, and His power and truly have an abundant life (John 10:10).

God desires for you to love Him above all so that you can live an overcoming life in Christ—a life of service for others, a life filled with purpose and meaning.

GOD'S NAMES FULL OF PROMISES

1. THE LORD IS EVER-PRESENT TO HELP

God is our refuge and strength,
a very present help in trouble.
PSALM 46:1

While life can be fragile and full of hard-ship, the Lord is present to help His people in times of trouble. Perhaps some imagine that God is unwilling to hear their prayers or unable to intervene, but the writer of this psalm saw reliance on God as essential. In fact, this dependence on God extends even into the extreme events of life such as an earthquake or a raging storm at sea. Those who learn to trust God as their strength and refuge have security in God from these highly dangerous and unpredictable events.

God does not necessarily promise deliverance from every dangerous event, but He is always present to strengthen His people. Moreover, God's presence is a source of security and strength, not a weak platitude or moral lesson. When people are held up by God's support, they will be certain of it. God's people are always secure in their position before the Lord, but there are times when God's intervention may look like comfort or confidence in the midst of hardship without the end of the hardship itself.

God's people today can trust that when life reaches its most tumultuous and uncertain points, the Lord stands beside His people. Wealth can evaporate with the loss of a job or a poor stock market. Home values can plummet. Powerful allies can switch allegiances. Even friends can move away or grow busy. The Lord does not grow weary of supporting His people and reassuring them, regardless of how trying their circumstances may have become.

PRAYER

God, You have promised to stand by us when our lives grow chaotic and even dangerous, providing a refuge to take shelter in and strength to face the challenges of life. May we rest in You today so that we will never boast of our own strength or neglect the precious gift of Your presence. Amen.

2. JESUS IS LORD OF LORDS

For he is Lord of lords, and King of kings:
and they that are with him are called,
and chosen, and faithful.
REVELATION 17:14

The book of Revelation uncovers several unusual and unsettling spiritual realities that show us how the forces of evil in the world fight against God and God's people. Rulers and authorities set themselves up against God and wage war in ways that are discouraging and disturbing. At times, it may even appear that the darkness has won. How can Jesus declare to anyone that He has overcome the world when so much evil appears to be at work?

In Revelation, John assures his readers that Jesus has conquered evil and that He will be revealed as the Lord over all other lords and the King over all other kings. There will come a day when God's power and presence will be unmistakable and supreme, even if there will be dark days until then.

What should God's people do in the midst of this uncertainty and ongoing spiritual struggle? The hope of God's people is to remain faithful, trusting in the message of Jesus and the words of scripture that have been passed down for generations. God's people are called and chosen. They are not forgotten or abandoned. Throughout suffering and the darkest of days, Jesus continues to stand by His people, even if His presence is difficult to discern in difficult or troubling times. John reminds God's people that their faithfulness and trust will not be in vain. As so much of the world is shaken and disrupted, there is hope for the people of God through the Lord of lords.

PRAYER

Jesus, You have conquered the principalities and powers in our world and established Yourself as the Lord who rules over every other lord. May we find rest today in Your power and position over our world, and may we remain among the faithful who put their trust in You. Amen.

3. THE LORD IS YOUR PROVIDER

*Consider the lilies of the field, how they grow;
they toil not, neither do they spin: and yet I say
unto you, that even Solomon in all his glory was
not arrayed like one of these. Wherefore, if God
so clothe the grass of the field, which to day is,
and to morrow is cast into the oven, shall he not
much more clothe you, O ye of little faith?*
MATTHEW 6:28–30

In times of uncertainty and lack, where are
you most likely to look for comfort and direction? Perhaps it's tempting to look at what
others have. There surely is no shortage of financial and business experts offering their best
tips and tricks for prosperity and purpose. They
have the simple plans and systems that anyone
can put into practice to find financial stability.

On the other hand, Jesus suggests that
you look outside to the flowers in the fields.
Rather than envying the bounty of others, Jesus asks that you consider how God has cared
for creation and brought about beauty in simple places. This is a different kind of provision
and beauty, but it is accessible to all and it is
renewed every day.

There is no end to the goals you could

meet. There is always another item you could purchase. There is always a home that offers a bit more space. There is always another task at work. Yet God gives the flowers whatever they need simply because they exist and He delights in them. Wouldn't God take much more delight in caring for His beloved children?

God's children can use this passage to consider the parts of their lives that need to be entrusted to God much like a flower in the field. Just as a flower rests in God's provision in whatever way it comes, you may have financial, career, or personal goals that need to be surrendered today. Perhaps you can cut off worry at the root as you gratefully focus on the blessings of God coming into bloom right now.

PRAYER

Father, You care for Your children and provide for their needs. Help us to entrust our worries and cares to You so that our faith will grow and we can live in gratitude for what we have. May we see Your provision today as we place our hope in You. Amen.

4. THE LORD IS YOUR HEALER

*Bless the LORD, O my soul, and forget not
all his benefits: who forgiveth all thine
iniquities; who healeth all thy diseases. . .*
PSALM 103:2–3

The story of scripture could be described as one of forgetfulness. The people of God had profound revelations and interactions with God, they forgot about God, and then the prophets came to remind them of God again. The cycle of forgetfulness continued throughout many centuries right through the time of Christ, and Christians today face the same struggle to remember the Lord's past works and many benefits.

Perhaps many have trouble remembering the Lord's past mercies and benefits because so many alternative sources of comfort are available. It's often easier to seek a distraction or comforting habit than to seek the Lord's comfort and healing. Going to God for healing requires seeing one's sickness with clarity and committing unflinchingly to the regular practice of repentance. There is a cost to this type of healing, but it is the deep restoration that is the birthright of every child of God. It is available to all who will take hold of it.

Those who have experienced the depths of God's grace and mercy are the least likely to forget about the healing power of God. They are the ones who sing God's praises and encourage others to run to God for the same healing and restoration.

While everyone falls into sin, the healing power of God remains for all who will remember it and take hold of it. Experiencing this redemptive power of God is a matter of recalling the mercy of God in the past that also extends to everyone who desires it today. Much as Jesus spoke of Himself as a physician who has come to heal the sick, God has long desired to heal His people from their sin.

PRAYER

Father, You generously forgive Your
people's sins and promise to heal all
of their afflictions completely. May we
confess our failings and trust our wounds
to Your care so that we may be fully
restored. May we remember Your mercies
today so that we remain near to You. Amen.

5. THE LORD IS YOUR BANNER

Thou hast given a banner to them that fear thee,
that it may be displayed because of the truth.
PSALM 60:4

In a time of suffering, uncertainty, and loss, God desires to be the rallying point for His people, setting up a banner of safety and security for them when disaster strikes. A time of crisis may prove to be the most revealing moment in showing where God's people have placed their trust. People set up all kinds of safety nets, from financial protections, to security systems, to personal networks, all of which can provide a measure of shelter in their own right.

However, none of these banners are fully adequate to provide protection in a truly life-altering crisis or a time of loss. Today is the day to see the reality of God's presence in the world and to respond to Him with a healthy respect and fear, recognizing Him as the Creator of the world and the Sustainer of His people. Just as the people of Israel confessed their failures and faithlessness, there is time today for God's people to confess their misplaced trust and inadequate safety nets.

A time of loss and suffering can upend fragile security networks and demolish hope for the future. Only God can look ahead into the lives of His people and promise restoration, justice, and His comforting presence. In fact, the one certainty in this life is the presence of God. His banner has been extended for all to see. Those whose hearts are hardened against Him will seek their own protection and security, but those who rest in Him will find a ready support in their time of need.

PRAYER

Father, help us to see the false security networks we've set up, the ways we rely on our own resources, and the ways we turn to others for wisdom and guidance instead of to You and Your Spirit. Open our eyes to Your banner of protection and send Your Spirit to renew our minds and soften our hearts to Your message. Amen.

6. THE LORD SANCTIFIES YOU

And ye shall keep my statutes, and do them:
I am the LORD which sanctify you.
LEVITICUS 20:8

Much was at stake for the people of God when they entered a covenant with the Lord. They were called to a higher standard of holiness than their neighbors, but the benefits of these laws and statutes were clear and easy to see. The Lord's laws helped the people of Israel live at peace with each other and to do justice to others in their community, but more importantly, the law of the Lord enabled them to live at peace with God. A holy God desired to be with His people, but only if they were willing to abide by His teachings.

While the Lord challenged Israel to live in holiness and to adhere to a higher standard than their neighbors, He also made a significant promise that no one should overlook in the midst of the laws and decrees of Leviticus: the Lord promised to sanctify His people. The Lord is not disconnected from His people and their struggles to obey His law. He is invested in sanctifying them, remaining present for them as they seek to do what is right or when they repent for failing.

It's easy to focus on the laws and punishments of Leviticus and miss the good news for the people of God. The Lord desires holy and faithful people. This isn't a disconnected deity. For people struggling to leave their own selfish desires, plans, or "idols" of success and prosperity behind, the Lord promises His sanctification. The ministry of Jesus became the fulfillment of this promise made long ago.

PRAYER

Father, our lives are open before You. You know our failures and our desires. You know what holds us back from Your love and Your best plans for us and our neighbors. We trust You to sanctify us and to change us. Help us to pursue obedience and justice today. Amen.

7. THE LORD GIVES YOU PEACE

Peace I leave with you, my peace I give unto you: not as the world giveth, give I unto you. Let not your heart be troubled, neither let it be afraid.
JOHN 14:27

The disciples of Jesus were facing the terrifying prospect that their Teacher would be killed. Where would they go next? Who would lead them from that point on? They had left behind everything to follow Jesus, and their hearts were understandably troubled by the thought of losing Him.

As they pondered the unthinkable, Jesus assured them that He would give them a lasting peace that was unlike anything the world had ever seen. His peace would comfort their troubled hearts, speak to their growing fears, and leave them grounded in the reality of God's presence and power. While everything around them appeared chaotic and on the brink of collapse, Jesus assured them that He could overcome their fears and uncertainties.

On the other side of Jesus's death and resurrection, that promise of presence and peace remains. Those living in fear with troubled hearts have nothing to be ashamed of, as even the disciples who had Jesus standing next to them lived with great terror at the thought of the future. From the disciples on down to the followers of Jesus today, the promise of peace and comfort persists. Today is the day to open up to the peace of Jesus, to receive it, and to hold on to it in trust and faith.

Troubles will come. There will always be plenty to fear in this world. With each day's renewed struggles and worries, Jesus offers an invitation to receive Him and His comfort. This comforting presence won't stop the worst from happening as the disciples found out, but when God's power is present, there is always hope of resurrection and restoration.

PRAYER

Father, I bring today's fears and uncertainties to You, knowing that You care deeply for Your children and that You promise them peace. Just as You brought peace and comfort to Your disciples in their time of need, I trust You to help me remain grounded in the stability of Your loving presence. Amen.

8. THE LORD LEADS YOU TO SAFETY

In his days Judah shall be saved, and Israel shall dwell safely: and this is his name whereby he shall be called, THE LORD OUR RIGHTEOUSNESS.
JEREMIAH 23:6

Throughout a season of loss, insecurity, and fear about the future, the people of Israel received an assurance that God would one day restore them to peace, justice, and safety. God's righteous character isn't just a spiritual matter. It's tied in with His desire for justice and peace in the world. While the Israelites lived in captivity, the Lord assured them of future deliverance and salvation through a descendant of David. Their hopes and plans for the future were most likely far too small.

The Lord will bring about deliverance for His people one day, and so the challenge may be how to live with hope and faithfulness in the present. The time of waiting for the Lord to act and to bring deliverance, peace, safety, or holiness is where faith takes hold. Is God's promise enough?

The people of Israel had to wait many long years for God to act on their behalf and to free them from their captivity. The time of waiting is never easy, and it may be far longer than desired. Yet when God gives His people a promise, He is faithful not only to follow through but to provide in ways that are surprising and far more complete than what could be imagined. Many who are facing uncertainty and even suffering in the future may need to spend time asking what promise God is making them, what hope God is offering, and how they can wait patiently for God's coming restoration.

PRAYER

Holy Lord, You are faithful to fulfill Your promises and to lead Your people to restoration and peace. Give us eyes to see Your past faithfulness and ears to hear Your promises as they come to us. Give us the courage and faith to stand fast throughout our trials and difficulties as we wait for Your deliverance. Amen.

9. THE LORD SHEPHERDS YOU

The LORD is my shepherd; I shall not want.
He maketh me to lie down in green pastures:
he leadeth me beside the still waters.
He restoreth my soul: he leadeth me in the
paths of righteousness for his name's sake.
PSALM 23:1–3

David's psalm makes the striking admission that most people will not seek out or find still waters on their own. If they do find green pastures, they will not lie down in them without some prompting. Why is this the case? It may have something to do with the shepherd in charge of their lives.

Those who take an honest look at the results of their lives may find who their shepherd is sooner rather than later. Those who struggle to find peace, rest, or contentment may be looking to the "shepherds" of wealth, prosperity, fame, entertainment, power, or pleasure. These false shepherds never lead to security or hope for the future. They will not lead to a sense of peace or a restored soul. They are a stark contrast to the way the Lord leads His people.

God's people can find rest and tranquility

when they recognize they are lost on their own and have followed the wrong shepherds for too long. The Lord is a shepherd who cares for His sheep and promises to lead them to places of peace, contentment, and restoration, but these are hardly the same as fame, prosperity, or comfort, the goals of this world after which so many people chase. The Good Shepherd will make His name great by guiding His people and showing them how to live in holiness. Those who feel the need for direction, restoration, or serenity have the promise of the Good Shepherd who can lead them to the still waters and green pastures they may never find or enjoy on their own.

PRAYER

Loving Shepherd, You have laid down Your life for us and promised to lead us toward restoration and peace. Help us to recognize the false shepherds that have guided us astray, and give us the direction we need to find our way today so that we will choose the paths of righteousness. Amen.

10. THE LORD IS GLORIOUS

*If thou wilt not observe to do all the words
of this law that are written in this book,
that thou mayest fear this glorious and
fearful name, THE LORD THY GOD. . .*
DEUTERONOMY 28:58

The Lord is able to cause nations to rise and fall based on their obedience and humility. At a time when the people of Israel felt powerless and uprooted while wandering in the wilderness, the Lord reminded them of His glorious power and fearful name: those who obeyed His commands would be blessed and safe, while those who broke His commands would suffer punishment and curses. The list of blessings is wonderful and encouraging, while the list of curses is sobering. Whatever happened in the future, the Lord wanted Israel to know that no other deity could rescue them or guarantee their future.

The Israelites eventually abandoned the promises of God, seeking their own plans, goals, and desires. Like the nations around them, they tried to hedge their bets by worshipping other deities, and they made alliances with people who didn't share the same regard for the glorious name of God. Over time, these small and large compromises added up. The Israelites lost sight of their unique calling before God, and their God became just another deity among a pantheon of false gods who promised peace and prosperity.

The Lord is merciful and just, but He will not preserve His people from calamity forever. Those in search of God today should take note, lest they wander away from God's holy path and life-giving commandments. They may soon find themselves on their own, cut off from the all-powerful God who desires to make them His treasured possession. In seeking to increase their security and comfort, they begin to lose sight of God's promises and power.

PRAYER

Glorious God, help us to see both Your power and Your compassion, Your zeal for Your people and Your justice. Uproot the hold of sin in our lives. Expose the ways we fail to see You as You truly are. May we humbly seek and find You today so that we will remain mindful of Your power. Amen.

11. THE LORD OF HOSTS BLESSES THOSE WHO TRUST IN HIM

*O LORD of hosts, blessed is the
man that trusteth in thee.*
PSALM 84:12

The long-term benefits of trusting God and dwelling in God's presence may be hard to appreciate in the short term. It's one thing to look back at time spent in God's presence and to see the joy, peace, and blessings that have grown from it. In the short term, however, seeing the ways that God may be at work is more difficult. In the urgency of the moment, it's tempting to seek solutions, to work harder, and to keep moving at a faster pace. Once a faster lifestyle becomes the norm, it's hard to know when or even how to stop.

The psalmist writes that those who dwell in God's presence will find blessings and joy. Those who spend a day in the house of God are better off than those who spend a thousand days among those at the mercy of their own desires and sinful acts. The peace and joy of God's people are a result of where they spend their time. God's mercy is a pure gift of grace, but it is one that can certainly be neglected. Real joy, peace, and provision can be experienced by God's people, but first they must examine where they spend their time and in whom they put their trust.

God never desires to withhold any gifts from His people. His generous presence is there for them. They can bring their needs to Him without reservation. In God's presence, they will find the stability and support they need, as well as a joy that no one can take away.

PRAYER

Father, You have graciously made Yourself available and present. You have generously given Your Spirit to Your people so that we may fully enjoy Your loving presence, provision, and peace as we rest in You. Show us the distractions and priorities that get in the way of fully trusting You. Amen.

12. THE LORD IS THE HIGH, EXALTED GOD

Be still, and know that I am God: I will be exalted among the heathen, I will be exalted in the earth.
PSALM 46:10

Living out one's faith may require taking a leap of faith or making a life decision that may be disruptive or difficult. Other times, less action is needed and more stillness before God is preferred. In fact, daily stillness before God may be one of the most important "actions" for God's people.

Stillness before God acknowledges that infinite human activity simply isn't enough and can never be enough. It is a way of handing over trust to God on a regular basis, waiting to see God act rather than relying on human wisdom or plans. For people who are especially driven and adopt a Martha-like approach to solving their problems or tackling their daily schedule, stillness may be an even more important discipline. Regular times of stillness can stretch and grow one's faith in surprising ways.

Perhaps the most surprising result of stillness before God is the opportunity to watch God work. Do God's people believe that remaining still before God will really make a difference? The writer of this psalm is certain of it. The outcome of stillness before God is the exaltation of God among all people and nations. The more that God's people step out of the way, the more opportunities there are for God to move in fresh, noticeable ways. Moreover, for Christians who are concerned about sharing their faith, a time of stillness may give them a new way to testify to God's power and presence in the world.

PRAYER

Father, You have generously promised to be present in the lives of Your people and to work on their behalf when they remain still before You. Give us the grace to hold fast before Your loving presence and to wait with patience and faith as You intervene in our lives. Amen.

13. THE LORD IS THE GOD WHO SEES YOU

And [Hagar] called the name of the LORD that
spake unto her, Thou God seest me: for she said,
Have I also here looked after him that seeth me?
GENESIS 16:13

People can come up with plenty of reasons to skip prayer or to believe their prayers won't be heard by God. Yet the Bible is full of stories in which people who appeared to be outside of God's chosen people or uninvolved in God's plans called out to God. In each case, God heard and responded to those who called out in faith. The reality that is easy to overlook is that God is not the One who comes up with reasons to ignore prayers. If anything, God finds ways to respond to people from all backgrounds and experiences.

Hagar was desperate. She had nowhere else to turn. This was a moment of crisis in which she turned to God as a last resort. Nevertheless, God heard her and intervened on behalf of her and her child. A cry to God in a moment of crisis is easily written off as insincere. Do these moments truly matter to God?

In this story, God is seeking any opportunity

to meet with Hagar. Her desperation in this moment provides a chance for God to reveal Himself to her and even to make His name known beyond His chosen people. A low point or crisis is just one way for people to take a step toward deeper intimacy with God. God isn't keeping track of the circumstances, only the sincerity of heart of those who seek Him.

The grace of God is abundant and surprising. To anyone asking, "Does God see me?" or "Does God care about me?" this story replies with a striking affirmation: He most certainly does.

PRAYER

God, You see Your people in moments of joy, times of trial, and experiences of deep despair. Open our eyes to see how You are with us today so that we may enjoy Your presence, participate in Your work, and testify to others about Your generosity and goodness. Amen.

14. THE LORD IS THE EVERLASTING GOD

*And Abraham planted a grove in
Beersheba, and called there on the
name of the Lord, the everlasting God.*
GENESIS 21:33

While living in the land of the Philistines as a stranger, Abraham dug a well and planted a grove of trees as an act of faith that God had given him this land as his possession. Although his land was disputed by others, he set aside a place to pray and called on the name of the Lord.

In the present moment, Abraham's situation wasn't ideal. He had to pay for the land that God had granted him. Rivals surrounded him and powerful rulers and kings could take everything away from him without warning. It took faith to plant himself in this new land given to him by God. How could he find hope for the future when everything seemed stacked against him?

By creating a space to seek the Lord in the land promised to him, Abraham acknowledged that the "everlasting God" would be around far longer than the Philistines who surrounded him.

God would be able to follow through on His promises and to expand from the small grove of trees and the well that Abraham had established. His future was firmly in God's hands even when he faced enemies all around him.

When life becomes overwhelming or hopeless, remember that God outlasts the problems of this week, this month, and this year. God can cause a small act of faith to take root, grow, and become established in ways that exceed all expectations. The daily practice of seeking God, setting aside a space to meet with the Lord, acknowledges that the hope of God's people rests in the faithfulness of the Lord, not in the forces and powers that appear to be in control.

PRAYER

Father, You are the everlasting God who outlasts all worldly influencers and powers. You reward Your people for their faithfulness and trust. We trust You to guide us out of the depths of despair and the challenges that appear hopeless. May our faithfulness each day lead us to a place of rest in You. Amen.

15. THE LORD IS A MIGHTY WARRIOR

Ah Lord GOD! Behold, thou hast made the heaven and the earth by thy great power and stretched out arm, and there is nothing too hard for thee: thou shewest lovingkindness unto thousands, and recompensest the iniquity of the fathers into the bosom of their children after them: the Great, the Mighty God, the LORD of hosts, is his name.
JEREMIAH 32:17–18

The power of God extends throughout the earth and the sky, touching generations and impacting those who are faithful and faithless. Jeremiah reminded the people of Israel that they had completely underestimated the impact of their faithfulness on future generations. Their actions today had implications for the generations who followed them, setting them up for failure or blessings. The stakes of each generation's actions extend far beyond the day-to-day or even a few years. God can take the faithfulness of today and extend its impact far into the future.

Jeremiah composed this passage during a siege in which the loss of Jerusalem and the land of Israel to the Babylonians was guaranteed by God. It was a particularly hopeless situation.

The future appeared bleak. However, the Lord prompted Jeremiah to buy a field with the hope that the people of Israel would one day return to it.

Just as God created this world, so too can God bring renewal through those who are willing to trust in Him even in the darkest of times. The hope of God's people isn't just a matter of seeing what God can do in the present. The spiritual battles won today that result in renewal and transformation will be passed on in the future, just as the spiritual losses of today will extend to future generations to their detriment. In the midst of these high stakes, God's loving kindness and power offer reassurance that God is deeply invested in blessing His people.

PRAYER

Father, You are powerful and capable, able to bless and restore Your people for generations. Those who trust in You are promised that You are faithful and just. I bring my discouragement and despair to You, trusting that You are able to overcome and conquer, bringing hope and blessings in the future. Amen.

PROMISES OF LOVE AND SALVATION

16. GOD LOVES YOU IMMENSELY

For God so loved the world, that he gave his only begotten Son, that whosoever believeth in him should not perish, but have everlasting life.
JOHN 3:16

Nicodemus approached Jesus with the hope of unlocking the secrets to everlasting life, but as Jesus explained that he must be born again, he got lost in the details. After asking Jesus how a person could be literally "born again" as an adult, Nicodemus then learned about the deeper spiritual truths that formed the heartbeat of Jesus' ministry. God had sent Jesus into the world out of His deep love for people, that they might enjoy everlasting life. Jesus cut right to the chase, inviting Nicodemus to believe in Him and to look toward God's love for the world.

Perhaps it's tempting today to get lost in the details or particulars of Jesus' teachings. While He shared plenty of stories, parables, signs, and symbols, the core of His message took His listeners back to the sacrificial love of God. God's desire to save people from their destructive desires and plans prompted Jesus to come and offer His life. Jesus' mission was never to condemn people but to extend an invitation to experience the love of God. As Christians seek God in prayer, the study of scripture, or public worship, the reason for their access to God is the love of God, not anything they can do to change God's mind about them. Just as Nicodemus didn't have to understand the precise details of Jesus' message to believe in Him, Christians today don't have to understand how they are born again or why God loves them in order to experience His salvation.

PRAYER

Father, this world is Your beloved creation, and You desire that no one should perish. May I experience Your loving presence and sacrificial love today. May the presence of Jesus remind me that I am Your beloved child, saved from the destructive forces of this world by His life, death, and resurrection. Amen.

17. GOD LOVED YOU BEFORE THE WORLD BEGAN

According as he hath chosen us in him before the foundation of the world, that we should be holy and without blame before him in love.
EPHESIANS 1:4

This promise for God's people may appear too good to be true, and it's one that Paul leads off with for the sake of His readers. God's salvation extends back to the foundation of the world. The Lord desired to save His creation right from the start—intimacy with God was always the goal. The love of God that prompted the creation of the world runs through the creation of His people and extends right into the present where they are assured of being adopted into God's family.

This love for God's people is a promise that can be counted on and rested in. It's a source of hope that reaches into the here and now. The same God who chose the Ephesian believers continues to call out to those who hear and read about His love. There is nothing anyone can do to become a beloved child of God. It is a pure grace brought about by God's good pleasure and desire for communion with His people.

For everyone who feels distant from God or incapable of measuring up to the high calling of God's children, this scripture promises grace and adoption into God's family based on the goodness and will of God. This has been the plan since the foundation of the world. Those who put their hope in God find their true identities in Christ. By seeking Christ and resting in Christ's presence daily, they find the blessings and comfort of God's loving presence.

PRAYER

Loving Father, You have adopted us into Your family as part of Your plan since the founding of the world and have chosen us to be Your beloved children. May every other identity or illusion about ourselves and You fade away in the light of this reality. May we find rest and hope today in the presence of Christ alone.

18. GOD SAVES YOU FROM DESTRUCTION

The way of life is above to the wise,
that he may depart from hell beneath.
PROVERBS 15:24

The writer of Proverbs looked at two paths set before him: a way of wisdom and holiness before God and a way of foolishness that led to chaos and destruction. Translators have struggled to choose the best word for the Hebrew word *sheol* used in this verse, as it was used to mean the place of the dead. It typically had negative implications, but it wasn't exactly the same concept as "hell" as some understand it today. Some translators have even used the Hebrew word because they have been unable to find the English equivalent for it. Regardless, the truth remains that God's path of life is found through wisdom and not foolish indulgence and short-sighted gains in the present.

The promises of Proverbs repeatedly encourage readers to look beyond the urgency of the moment and the gains that can be found through impulsive decisions. Wisdom considers the long-term, even eternal implications of today's choices. Unfaithfulness in the small decisions today can add up and lead away from the path of wisdom. Wisdom does pay off in the long run, leading to greater peace with God and with others, as well as the hope of eternal life apart from the uncertainty, if not suffering, of "*sheol.*"

God desires for His people to choose the path of wisdom and has even promised the Holy Spirit as a guide to lead His people today. The same dangers remain today in pursuing the path of destruction, and the assistance of God has remained strong and certain.

PRAYER

Father, You desire that none should perish, and You sent Your Son in order to share Your divine wisdom through the presence of the Holy Spirit. Open our minds and spirits to Your wisdom and presence today so that we may be saved from the path of destruction, discover Your wisdom, and live in obedience to Your will. Amen.

19. JESUS SHOWS YOU THE FATHER

*Philip saith unto him, Lord, show us the
Father, and it sufficeth us. Jesus saith
unto him, Have I been so long time with
you, and yet hast thou not known me, Philip?
he that hath seen me hath seen the Father;
and how sayest thou then, Show us the Father?*
JOHN 14:8–9

Even the disciples, who lived with Jesus day-in-day-out, struggled to see the significance of His ministry and His identity with God the Father. They had direct access to the Father, but they didn't realize that Jesus was perfectly united with the Father as a member of the Trinity. If they wanted to know what God the Father was like, they only had to look at Jesus.

Jesus provided His disciples with unprecedented access to the Father and makes the same promise to all who follow Him today. The mercy and restoration of the Father are offered by grace right at this very moment to all who call on His name. It's possible that some have had negative experiences at churches or with certain Christians, and this has cast a cloud over their perception of God. Jesus aims to put those fears, uncertainties, and doubts to rest by assuring His followers that He and the Father are one. In fact, Jesus would not be able to perform so many compassionate miracles without the direct intervention of the Father.

This perfect unity with the Father pulls back the curtain between God and people. Jesus was fully God incarnate, united with the Father in purpose and love. Those who find Jesus and His ministry appealing have seen what God is truly like. Jesus' desire remains to draw all people to the Father. By sharing in His ministry today, Christians can both enter into this loving relationship with the Father and invite others to do the same.

PRAYER

Loving Father, You have revealed Your goodness and mercy through the ministry of Jesus. In Your perfect unity with Jesus the Son, You have given us hope to enter into Your rest and peace. May the ministry of Jesus bring Your healing into our lives so that our fears and uncertainties may be put to rest once and for all. Amen.

20. GOD MAKES YOU HIS CHILD

*But as many as received him, to them
gave he power to become the sons of God,
even to them that believe on his name.*
JOHN 1:12

The plan of salvation from the foundation of the world was to make people the children of God, adopting them into God's family on the basis of God's grace and mercy. This is a dramatic transformation through the power of God in the lives of ordinary people, calling them out of their everyday concerns and goals and giving them a new identity and direction in life. Stepping into this new identity is simple, and it is available to all. Yet the Gospel of John is a stark reminder that even the simple act of receiving a free gift from God can become complicated.

People were holding on to all kinds of other priorities and goals. The teachers of the law were confused and offended by Jesus. The people were obsessed with crowning Jesus as an earthly political king. The rulers were so paranoid about losing their power and influence that it was more convenient to make Jesus an enemy than to truly listen. The many large crowds who witnessed His miracles fled for their lives when Jesus was arrested because they feared losing their own lives. Yes, Jesus invites all to receive the gift of becoming a child of God, but so many things can obscure that gift.

God has come down to earth to save people; the hard work has already been done. God has come as our Savior, not as a judge who condemns. If God is already present and ready to save, then the way to participate in this new life is to receive it.

PRAYER

Lord Jesus, You have come down to make people Your own children and to welcome them into Your family. Help us to see what prevents us from receiving the free gift of Your grace, to leave our distractions behind, and to pursue the transforming love You share from the Father today.

21. GOD FORGIVES ALL YOUR SINS

*For as the heaven is high above the earth,
so great is his mercy toward them that fear
him. As far as the east is from the west, so far
hath he removed our transgressions from us.*
PSALM 103:11–12

It's easy to imagine the wrath and judgment of God because the sins and failures of the past often come to mind. Throughout the Bible, we see that the people of God could think of many reasons they were unworthy of God and of many ways they had failed. They had worshipped false gods, trusted in the help of pagan nations, and exploited the poor and vulnerable. They had looked everywhere for help except to the Lord their God. When calamity struck, they often returned to God in repentance, but would they ever be received by God when they finally did confess their sins?

Today's psalm offers a striking image of God removing the transgressions of His people to the greatest extreme imaginable—sending them away as high as the heavens and from one extreme of the horizon to another. When God sees His people, their sins are nowhere in sight. The people are all God sees. God's mercy is an act of pure grace and compassion that is complete and thorough.

There are no half measures or changes to God's mercy. Their sins are gone for good, and their hope for the future is grounded in their complete separation from their past. It no longer has to hold them back and prompt them to hide in shame. God's mercy has won complete victory. Hope for the future is based not on anyone's ability to obey but on God's power to bring healing and transformation among people who have been saved from their sins.

PRAYER

*Father, You have separated Your people
from their sins so that You can see them
in the perfection and holiness of Your Son.
May we find the peace and confidence of Your
redemptive work today as we approach You in
prayer and bring our requests to You. May our
position before You provide comfort. Amen.*

22. THE SPIRIT ASSURES
YOU OF SALVATION

And he that keepeth his commandments
dwelleth in him, and he in him. And hereby
we know that he abideth in us, by the
Spirit which he hath given us.
1 JOHN 3:24

Where can the followers of Jesus find their assurance of salvation? The sign from God isn't typically a mountaintop experience or a booming voice from a cloud. The assurance God provides is developed over the long term as a Christian lives a life of obedience. The key isn't that someone has been obedient or followed God's commands per se. Assurance comes from the driving force in the Christian's life that makes holiness and obedience possible. Willpower alone is not enough to enable a believer to live in holiness or to be set apart as God's child. In fact, such willpower is no assurance at all for a Christian's security, since moral failure and sin are always a possibility. God provides a deeper, lasting promise of security for the salvation of His people.

By dwelling in God and abiding in God's Spirit, Christians will see the gradual transformation of their lives. They will see the fruits of the Spirit that they could never produce on their own. The desire to keep God's commands will grow stronger and take root in their lives so that transformation becomes a natural out-growth of the Spirit's work.

Over time, the work of God in the life of the Christian becomes evident, and this deep-rooted stability in the Spirit becomes a source of comfort and assurance. It could even be argued that this deeper stability is more secure than a voice from a cloud or a momen-tary spiritual epiphany that could be explained away or even forgotten. Christians have the greater promise of God's lifelong presence and ongoing transformation that becomes their assurance and security.

PRAYER

Jesus, You have sent Your Spirit into our lives to cleanse us from sin, to reform the desires of our hearts, and to bring about the desire to live in obedient communion with You and with Your church. Turn our attention to Your Spirit's presence today so that we may learn what it is to abide in You. Amen.

23. GOD HELPS YOU TO FORGIVE OTHERS

And when ye stand praying, forgive, if ye have ought against any: that your Father also which is in heaven may forgive you your trespasses.
MARK 11:25

As Jesus told His listeners to think about prayer in larger terms, believing in God's ability to move mountains and gaining confidence to make bold requests of God, He provided a simple way to check whether they had fully grasped the depths of God's forgiveness for them. It wasn't enough for them to believe in God's power to perform great miracles. They were also called to believe in God's power to forgive sins. Those who were unable to forgive others were in danger of missing the depth of God's forgiveness.

Jesus taught that those who had been forgiven much would also forgive much. Therefore, those who entered prayer while bearing a grudge against others had set up a serious barrier between themselves and God. Either they were unaware of God's forgiveness for them or they were failing to show the same mercy of God toward others. In either case, it's hard to imagine someone praying while either failing to grasp the mercy of God or holding on to a grudge toward another person.

God's mercy and forgiveness are given to anyone who repents, and there is a good reason for this order in prayer. Sin and resentment prevent people from seeing God clearly and abiding in His presence. These become distractions and barriers to God. Failing to see God's mercy also presents a practical barrier, limiting how someone may pray. Can those who pray truly open themselves up in trust and surrender to God if they fail to see His mercy and forgiveness with clarity?

PRAYER

Father, You have forgiven us of our sins and promised us restoration through Jesus. May we understand the depths of Your mercy and forgiveness today so that we can approach You in prayer without reservation or hesitation. May we extend the same mercy and forgiveness to others as well. Amen.

24. IF YOU SEEK GOD, YOU'LL FIND HIM

*But if from thence thou shalt seek the L*ORD
thy God, thou shalt find him, if thou seek
him with all thy heart and with all thy soul.
DEUTERONOMY 4:29

At the lowest point for the people of Israel, the Lord offered them hope for the future. All would not be lost even if they trusted in other gods, suffered defeat on the battlefield, saw the Lord's temple destroyed, and were sent off into exile. Even if they were suffering the consequences of their sins, God could not forget His people. They were never cut off from God's covenant even if they had abandoned God's commands or the type of life God's people were expected to live.

On the other side of disobedience, calamity, and exile, the Lord offered His people the hope of restoration if they made a single but significant change to their lives. They could no longer divide their loyalties. They had to be fully committed to the search for God, not divided in their priorities or allegiances. The problem throughout the history of Israel was that in any pursuit of God the people still sought other deities and sources of comfort and deliverance. They weren't seeking the Lord with all of their hearts.

Those who would fully commit themselves to the pursuit of the Lord, however, were promised that they would find Him. Even with their past failures and divisions, they were assured that God could still be found. They still had hope because of God's mercy. God was not playing hard to get with His people. Rather, they were unable to see God with clarity. Those who seek will find, provided they seek with all of their hearts.

PRAYER

Father, You desire full communion and peace with Your people, promising that You can be found by all who commit to finding You. Reveal the divisions and distractions in our hearts that keep us from finding You. May we find You today as we approach You in prayer with a united desire to be fully present to You and Your mercy. Amen.

25. GOD HELPS YOU TO OBEY HIM

If ye love me, keep my commandments.
JOHN 14:15

Jesus sought to revolutionize the way people come to know God and live in obedience. He revealed the love and generosity of God the Father to all people, inviting all who are willing to join in the loving relationship of the Father and the Son. Most importantly, Jesus promised the Holy Spirit to those who sought Him and lived in obedience. The basis of Jesus' ministry was always love.

Love, not fear, duty, or obligation, drives Jesus' call for obedience. He didn't ask for honor or reverence. He asked His followers to live in the love that He showed them. As He modeled His love for them throughout His ministry, Jesus asked them to do the same in return. This obedience to the commands of Jesus ensured they could receive the presence of the Holy Spirit and enjoy the security of His promises. The Spirit would guide and direct them, helping them find their way in the years to come.

There is a consistent simplicity to the message of Jesus that is easy for readers to miss. Jesus taught that the first and greatest command is to love the Lord with heart, mind, soul, and strength. While obedience to His commands is important, He wanted His followers to be driven by love. Perhaps the greatest barrier for many when it comes to obedience today is whether people believe that God loves them. Obedience should be the sign that God's people know they are loved and are reciprocating that love.

PRAYER

Jesus, You have revealed Your love by walking among us, bearing our sorrows, and revealing the love of the Father to us. May we experience Your love today and live in faithful obedience to Your commands so that we can participate in the full joy of Your indwelling Holy Spirit. Amen.

PROMISES OF THE HOLY SPIRIT

26. YOU PARTAKE OF
GOD'S RIGHTEOUSNESS

*And it shall be our righteousness, if we observe
to do all these commandments before the
Lord our God, as he hath commanded us.*
DEUTERONOMY 6:25

The future generations in Israel would need to learn about the laws of God, and they surely would have questions about why they had to behave differently than the other nations. Why would they have to observe so many commands? Why did their conduct come under greater scrutiny? Why was their worship limited so dramatically compared to the people who relied on many different deities? These were valid questions for people who were expected to adopt values and practices that were quite different from those of every other people.

The book of Deuteronomy teaches that God's laws were a reminder that the Israelites had been chosen by God to be set apart. God had delivered His people from bondage in Egypt and given them a land to live in.

Remaining in that land under God's protection depended in part on their faithfulness to God, trusting in God's laws and following the paths God had set before them. God's saving message to other nations depended on the ability of His people to obey Him and to participate in His righteousness.

Ultimately, the future of people today also hinges on how well older generations pass along the commands and teachings of scripture to their children. Those who want to be among God's set-apart people have a mission to pass that holy calling on to their children. Those who obey the commands of God will be declared righteous before God and will enjoy the security of God's presence. Those who depart from God's commands are leaving behind not only the holy calling they have but also God's righteous calling for their children.

PRAYER

Father, You have called us to be set apart, to be holy and to participate in Your righteousness so that we can serve as a sign of Your salvation to all people. May we live in humble surrender and obedience to You so that we can participate in Your righteousness and share it with others. Amen.

27. YOU PARTAKE OF GOD'S HOLINESS

And that ye put on the new man,
which after God is created in
righteousness and true holiness.
EPHESIANS 4:24

Paul contrasted the two ways of living in his letter to the Ephesians. One way involves ignorance, complete indulgence, and a hardening toward the life of God. It is focused on the needs of self and doesn't take account of the consequences of selfish choices. Those who choose this path walk in darkness and are unable to grasp the wisdom of God. However, those who are in Christ can choose to leave that way of life behind. They can benefit from the wisdom of God if they step back from their acts of selfish indulgence.

The point that Paul makes here is essential: Christians can choose to put on a new self, but that new self has been created by God. They don't create the self that they put on. God has given the new self to them as a gift.

God offers His people the opportunity to be renewed and changed, but partaking in this new identity in Christ depends on getting two parts right. First, God's people must break away from their life of sin; and second, they must choose to turn toward God. However, it's not up to them to weave a new identity in Christ from scratch. That's where the Spirit's power goes to work in their lives.

The new self resembles its Creator, bearing the image of God's righteousness and holiness. There is a resemblance to God in the new person because God's power has been turned loose in those who turn to God.

PRAYER

Jesus, You offer Your people renewal and deliverance from sin if they choose to turn away from it and put on the new life You offer them. Help us to see the sins that hinder us, and give us faith to believe that Your Spirit is at work in us to create a new life patterned after Your holiness and righteousness. Amen.

28. GOD'S HOLY SPIRIT
LIVES IN YOU

*But the Comforter, which is the Holy Ghost,
whom the Father will send in my name, he shall
teach you all things, and bring all things to your
remembrance, whatsoever I have said unto you.*
JOHN 14:26

Jesus gave His followers the seemingly impossible task of carrying on His ministry, teaching others with His same wisdom and insight while also performing miracles and signs that rivaled His own. How could anyone possibly take on the ministry of Jesus without expectations of failure? How could they ever keep all of His teachings straight when He was gone when they still misunderstood so much when they spoke with Him day after day?

The hope for Jesus' followers and all who have come after them is that the Holy Spirit was given to them as a source of insight, wisdom, and remembrance, enabling them to keep the teachings of Jesus straight. They would not be left alone to carry on Jesus' ministry. The Spirit of God, who was with Jesus throughout His ministry, would be passed along to them as well. They would have access to the teaching ministry of the Spirit as they stepped out to share the message of Jesus and to carry on His work among the people.

God's people are not left alone to find their way. They don't have to rely on their own wisdom and learning, even if these things are not bad by themselves. The ministry of Jesus continues today because the Holy Spirit remains among God's people and empowers them to imitate the ministry of Jesus. Moreover, Jesus knew that hard times would come to His followers. Thus, the Holy Spirit came not just with power but with comfort to help His followers endure the hard times ahead.

PRAYER

Jesus, You have promised us that the Holy Spirit will offer comfort, wisdom, and insight to our ministry today. Help us to carry on Your ministry to others by yielding to the guidance of the Holy Spirit. May our words and actions benefit from the Spirit's presence and activity in our lives. Amen.

29. GOD GIVES YOU GREAT LOVE

But God commendeth his love toward us, in that, while we were yet sinners, Christ died for us.
ROMANS 5:8

In a moment of weakness and failure, many people are tempted to believe that they are unworthy of God. They may believe they are unable to approach a holy God in a state of disobedience. However, Paul offers hope for all who will acknowledge their need for God: Christ died for sinners before they had even repented.

What do sinners need to change about themselves to make God love them? According to Paul: nothing. God's love and compassion for people prompted Jesus to come to earth, suffering death before rising again. Paul frequently wrote about the height, depth, and width of God's love, challenging his readers to stop disqualifying themselves from the love of God.

The first move belongs to God. While people are expected to respond to the overtures of God's love, nothing is holding people back from God other than their own sense of unworthiness. Jesus died for people while they were at their worst in order for God to turn them into His own holy and beloved people.

God is so unlike people that the truth of His great love is still surprising and unexpected for most people. Paul writes that even if it's rare for someone to die for the sake of a good person, God was willing to die for the salvation of sinful people. This is a kind of mercy and sacrifice that the weak and sinful surely don't expect, but entering into the rest and salvation of God is a matter of accepting this radical, unearned grace and forgiveness.

PRAYER

Jesus, You came to die for us while we were yet sinners who worked against Your good purposes and plans for our world. Open our eyes to the depths of Your love and mercy so that we can approach You with boldness and confidence. May we gratefully share the message of Your salvation with others today. Amen.

30. GOD FILLS YOU WITH HIS SPIRIT

For ye are bought with a price:
therefore glorify God in your body,
and in your spirit, which are God's.
1 CORINTHIANS 6:20

Christians are promised that they belong to the body of Christ and have the Spirit dwelling within them. This unity with Christ and with the Spirit is the great hope and promise of Christians for salvation, not to mention peace with God today. Yet such unity also carries important implications for how believers live each day. Those united with Christ share in His body, and He is united with their bodies as well. This is especially important for matters of sexual morality, since Paul teaches that Christians should use their bodies to glorify God, not to indulge their passions and desires without limitations.

The Corinthians were especially prone to indulging themselves, disconnecting spiritual realities from their physical actions. However, Paul sees the human body and human spirit as closely linked together. The actions of the body have spiritual implications, just as the spiritual work of Christ has physical implications for Christians. Christ sacrificed His own body so that they could join Him as members of God's family.

Taking up the imagery of a temple where people go to worship, Paul challenged his readers to view their own bodies as a sacred space that is set apart for God. The actions they took in prayer or service to others could be considered offerings much like someone would offer at the temple. Their desire to live in obedience to God could be considered an act of reverence that worshippers would show at the temple. Acts that glorified God through their bodies became the new normal for the people of God.

PRAYER

Jesus, You have joined us into Your body as one with You and sent Your Spirit to dwell in our lives. May we remember the sacrifice You made for us as we live each day aware of Your presence in our bodies and our joy of glorifying the Father in all we do. Amen.

31. GOD GIVES YOU THE
FRUIT OF THE SPIRIT

*For ye were sometimes darkness, but now
are ye light in the Lord: walk as children
of light: (For the fruit of the Spirit is in all
goodness and righteousness and truth;)
Proving what is acceptable unto the Lord.*
EPHESIANS 5:8–10

While everyone knows what it's like to live in the darkness apart from God, Christians have direct access to God the Father and the indwelling Holy Spirit because of Jesus. Christians can seek the direction of God in their daily choices and in their larger plans for life so that they can live in the clarity and peace of God's light. Paul doesn't mince words about the challenges that Christians face: there is great evil in the world. Many influences can drag Christians back into the confusion and obscurity of the darkness where it is difficult to live in obedience to God.

Consequently, Christians must continually bring their thoughts, plans, and actions into the light of God so that they can be shown for what they are and so that they can live in communion with God and the people of God. For people who are forgiven and redeemed from their sins, living in the light in this way is a guarantee of enjoying freedom from sin and holding on to hope when darkness threatens.

Christians can seek out what is pleasing to God by thinking about what is right, good, and true. What brings hope, peace, and restoration to this world? These are the things that are pleasing to God. In addition, Paul calls on his readers to expose the works of darkness with the light of God. This is a helpful exercise as well because it reveals the fruits or outcomes of sin. While people living in darkness may see only the benefits of indulgence or self-centeredness, Christians living in God's light can contrast the wisdom of God with the folly of the world.

PRAYER

Father, You have given us the gift of Your light and the wisdom of the Spirit to discern what is good and what is evil. Help us to see our actions and thoughts in the clarity of Your light so that we can seek Your good and perfect will today for the sake of Your glory and the good of our neighbors. Amen.

32. GOD GIVES YOU GIFTS OF THE SPIRIT

But the manifestation of the Spirit is given to every man to profit withal.
1 Corinthians 12:7

Every Christian has been enabled to serve others and to live in obedience because of the Holy Spirit's gifts. The gifts of the Holy Spirit build up the church and ensure the health of each member. While it may be tempting to look at spiritual gifts as a path to personal fulfillment and a way to fulfill one's destiny, the primary focus is on becoming more encouraging and constructive toward others.

No particular gift is any better than another. In fact, the Spirit is behind these different gifts to ensure that everyone's needs are met. No particular ministry or place is higher than another since the Spirit enables each gift and all the gifts serve the same God. As tempting as it is to elevate certain gifts or ministries over others, such an act misunderstands where these gifts come from and how they work. There is no hierarchy of importance within the plans of God. As each member of the church works together to serve others, those inside and outside the church experience the fullness of God's Spirit.

If Christians have found recognition or pride to be an issue in ministry, they may need to seek the Spirit's guidance. Have they overlooked certain gifts from the Spirit? Are there ways God is guiding them to serve in greater faith? Have they ruled out a particular ministry because of how they perceived themselves or that ministry? The gifts of the Spirit are intended to bring each member of the church into dependence on the Spirit so that they may serve others with confidence and peace.

PRAYER

Holy Spirit, You have given us gifts to serve others and abilities that are beyond our understanding. May we find peace in Your provision for us, confidence in Your power, and contentment in the results that Your gifts bring about in our service to others. Amen.

33. GOD GIVES YOU PEACE

*And the peace of God, which passeth
all understanding, shall keep your hearts
and minds through Christ Jesus.*
PHILIPPIANS 4:7

The peace that comes from God isn't a passing feeling or a fragile state of mind. Rather, the peace of God guards the hearts and minds of God's people. This peace of God is beyond understanding because it defies circumstances. When the peace of God has settled on His people, they are protected from the unexpected and the unsettling. That isn't to say they won't experience sadness or even fear. Rather, they will enjoy a sense of security that transcends their circumstances.

Where does this peace come from? According to Paul, peace doesn't come from circumstances or avoidance of the truth. Rather, peace comes from the regular practice of prayer, in which we trust God with the circumstances of life, express gratitude regularly, and make our needs known to God. These practices of surrender and gratitude place God in control as we look to Him for direction and guidance in the highs and lows of life.

The peace of God comes to those who think of how to get God more involved in the challenges of life rather than coming up with their own solutions and plans. There will be plenty of opportunities to focus on what's going badly or what hasn't happened in life, but praying with a spirit of surrender places control with God. This isn't some far-off promise reserved for only the ultraspiritual. Paul assured his readers that they should rejoice, for the Lord is near to them. God's people have a guarantee that they can bring their prayer requests to God in confidence.

PRAYER

Father, You are close to Your people and desire to pass along Your peace that defies all circumstances. May we bring our worship, gratitude, and supplications to You in complete confidence and hope so that we can experience Your peace that will guard our hearts and minds. Amen.

34. GOD GIVES YOU JOY

Thou wilt shew me the path of life: in thy
presence is fulness of joy; at thy right
hand there are pleasures for evermore.
PSALM 16:11

Everyone is tempted at some point to envy the possessions of others or to seek possessions beyond what one has. There's always a way to make an upgrade in life. Even the accomplishments or attributes of others can become a source of comparison and discontent. Achieving a certain level of success, power, or influence can become a lifelong distraction that leads people to run from one trend to another. This pursuit of growth, wealth, status, or success can be draining and leaves many alienated from God.

Today's psalm offers a different approach to the issues of life. Begin with contentment in God. Choose the Lord as the ultimate portion and goal in life and then accept where the boundary lines fall. The Lord is the heritage of His people, but seeing the benefits of that can be challenging when there are so many other measures for success and contentment. Throughout the many paths in life toward goals and accomplishments, today's psalm is a reminder that God directs His people toward a fulfilling and joyful life.

While it's tempting to seek joy in possessions, experiences, or accomplishments, the fullness of joy that everyone craves is found in God's presence. Taking time to sit in silence before God, to meditate on a psalm, or to read scripture is a step toward this joy, cultivating a space of rest and trust in the promises of God. For those who feel far from the pleasures of God or the peace of God's presence, today's psalm is a reminder to seek God's presence daily and to trust that God can cause the boundary lines of life to fall in pleasant places.

PRAYER

Lord, You have promised to show Your people the path of life, to share with them the fullness of Your joy, and to give them the pleasures of Your right hand. May we create time and space to meditate on scripture and to seek Your presence so that we can travel on Your path and experience Your promises. Amen.

35. GOD GIVES YOU A SOUND MIND

For God hath not given us the spirit of fear;
but of power, and of love, and of a sound mind.
2 TIMOTHY 1:7

As Timothy faced persecution and uncertainty, Paul reminded him that the gift of God's Spirit had been passed along to him when he laid hands on him. God's Spirit couldn't be revoked or lost, and external circumstances were not a sign of Timothy's failure or God's displeasure. Rather, the challenges he faced were an opportunity to return to the moment that he received God's Spirit. This was a time to look back in faith and to let that gift become rekindled within his spirit.

The source of someone's hope can be detected in their responses to the circumstances of life. God gives His people a spirit of power, love, and clarity of mind. The Spirit of God gives His people the ability to bear up under the frightening and challenging moments of life. The spirit of this world is one of fear, disorder, and hate. God does not give His people a spirit of fear.

For those who are fearful today, Paul's words are a reminder that fear does not come from God. God provides love, understanding, and strength to face the challenges of life. Whether God's people must seek out those who can pray for them or simply remember the blessings they have already received, the Spirit of God empowers them to overcome fear. Real peace of mind and hope are found when Christians trust in God's Spirit.

PRAYER

Father, You grant Your people love, strength, and a sound mind when others turn to fear and despair. May we remember the blessings of Your Spirit today so that we can live with confidence in times of uncertainty and love in times of hatred and anger. May Your Spirit guide and direct us today. Amen.

36. GOD GIVES YOU POWER

*The God of Israel is he that giveth
strength and power unto his people.*
PSALM 68:35

As the people of Israel faced uncertainty and threats, they could hedge their bets by worshipping a variety of different gods and making alliances with neighboring kings, or they could enter the sanctuary of God. By focusing on God alone, rather than the strength of their enemies or the other options available to them, the people of Israel had an opportunity to see the reality of God's power and might on their behalf. The more they served other gods or sought the help of neighboring powers, the less they saw God's power at work.

However, those who worshipped God understood that God had set the world in motion and that God stood above all people as King. This awesome God whom they worshipped in the sanctuary would demonstrate His power and might on their behalf in the days to come.

Times of trial and difficulty often reveal the source of one's hope and faith. The thing that sets the faithful apart from the faithless is never determined in the heat of the moment.

Rather, faith is grown and developed over time in worship. By seeking God regularly and contrasting God's power with the weaker forces of this world, the people of Israel were able to pray the words of this psalm with confidence. Christians today may not have a sanctuary to pray in, but they can create a space each day to focus on the power and faithfulness of God regardless of circumstances.

PRAYER

Lord, You created the world and keep it in motion through Your power and mercy. May we trust You to guide us through confusions, deliver us from evil, and lead us forward in hope. May we live in confidence in Your power and wisdom today. Amen.

37. GOD HELPS YOU WITNESS TO OTHERS

For I am not ashamed of the gospel of Christ: for it is the power of God unto salvation to every one that believeth; to the Jew first, and also to the Greek.
ROMANS 1:16

The power of God at work in Paul's life made him eager to share the Gospel message far and wide. As the Gospel took root in his life, he saw that it was intended for everyone, Jews and Gentiles; there were no exceptions to God's mercy. While the Gospel completely upended everything he thought he knew, prompting him to live differently and to face many enemies, Paul wasn't ashamed of the message of salvation that rescued people from separation from God. He knew the steep cost of disobedience and saw that God's righteousness was offered graciously as a gift to all.

For those who are uncertain how to share their faith or who maybe even harbor fears about sharing the Gospel message, Paul's path is an accessible and relatable one. Paul saw the power of God firsthand in his own life. He lived in its disruption, seeing so many things in his life change. In the end, though, Paul experienced the power of God's salvation and the hope of the Holy Spirit in his life. He didn't experience shame about the Gospel because he was living so completely in the hope of its message.

As he traveled from one town to another, he had a fire in his spirit about the ways he had experienced God's mercy. He had been saved from the folly of his sins and the coming judgment of God. Paul had experienced God's salvation so thoroughly that he didn't even have time to think of being ashamed.

PRAYER

Jesus, may we live in the hope and peace of Your righteousness today so that we can share Your Gospel message freely and without reservation. May the reminders of Your forgiveness and mercy always guide us toward boldness and clarity as we tell others about You. Amen.

38. GOD'S PLANS WILL NOT BE UNDERMINED

*Ask of me, and I shall give thee the heathen
for thine inheritance, and the uttermost
parts of the earth for thy possession.*
PSALM 2:8

This psalm, which was written for the king of Israel, puts the sociopolitical events of the psalmist's time into perspective. If this king rules over the nations, it is not because of his superior strength or wisdom. His success is tied with the will of God. God has placed the king over Israel and has set the terms of his kingdom: Remain obedient to God, and all shall go well for the king and the kingdom. Rather than relying on his own wisdom and power, he is told by God to simply ask for victory. God desired to establish a chosen people as a sign for all other nations, and the king played an important role in spreading that message to the ends of the earth.

As other kings or conspirators set up their plans to overtake the king, they overlooked the fact that God had a great plan for salvation, and the king of Israel had a critical part in that plan. Much like the advice from Gamaliel in Acts 5, any plan coming from God could not fail. If the king of Israel had God's blessing and backing, he need only ask God for victory. However, if he abandoned God or departed from God's ways, he would be in danger of undergoing the same fate as his enemies.

God desires to bless His people and to invite others to learn His ways. This psalm reminds readers that God's power should not be underestimated or overlooked. An appropriate response for God's people is awe at the privilege of taking part in God's redemption plan.

PRAYER

Lord, You have shown Your power and might to previous generations, causing kings to rise and fall according to Your purpose. May we remember and respect these stories of Your strength today and live in obedience so that we can play our part in sharing Your message with the world. Amen.

39. GOD TRANSFORMS YOU INTO CHRIST'S IMAGE

And we know that all things work together for good to them that love God, to them who are the called according to his purpose. For whom he did foreknow, he also did predestinate to be conformed to the image of his Son, that he might be the firstborn among many brethren.
ROMANS 8:28–29

God's goal for His people is transformation, re-creating them in the image of His Son so that they can continue the ministry of Jesus today. God doesn't let the circumstances of life hold people back from being counted among His family. While God doesn't want suffering or violence to happen among His people, He works through even the deepest pain of His people to bring about blessing and restoration.

The plan of salvation that was set in place long before God's people were born is stronger than the highs and lows of sin in this world. God has decreed that His people will be saved regardless of the hardships they have endured, the ways they have failed, or the suffering they may endure in the future. Just as Paul wrote that nothing can separate God's people from the love of Christ, nothing can undermine the plan to transform people into the children of God. God can redeem and transform everything.

Rather than asking what exactly God has predestined in each person's life, Paul appears to be far more concerned with saying that nothing can undermine the purpose of God in this world. Most importantly for the people of God, those who remain in Christ will be transformed into His image. Whatever they have been in the past will be overshadowed by the power of God. Through this transformation they will be empowered to reach out to many others, inviting them to experience God's presence for themselves.

PRAYER

Father, nothing can separate us from Your love and Your ultimate purposes of salvation and transformation. You take all that has happened to us and use it for our benefit. May Your power be at work in us as we abide in You and fulfill Your purpose for our lives. Amen.

PROMISES OF GUIDANCE AND WISDOM

40. GOD LEADS AND GUIDES YOU

I will lead them in paths that they have not known: I will make darkness light before them, and crooked things straight. These things will I do unto them, and not forsake them.
ISAIAH 42:16

When the people of Israel had chosen to follow other gods and disobeyed the Lord, they were promised that the Lord would lead them forward, healing their past failures. In places where there was no path forward, the Lord would guide them. In places where they saw only darkness, the Lord would provide light. Most significantly, for people who had known alienation from God, the Lord promised that their past unfaithfulness would not condemn them in the future. The Lord would not forsake them.

Isaiah promised that the deliverance of God would come as a kind of surprise that would give hope to the hopeless and direction to the directionless. In each place that appeared to be a dead end, the Lord would show them a path to take. This hope for the hopeless is a common theme throughout the Bible, with God promising hope to those who appeared to have no future.

Readers today may have little hope in their own wisdom or may be discouraged by their past failures. The key factor for them is the promise of God to intervene in their lives, carrying them when they are unable to move forward and shining light into the darkest places. At the same time, God promises to overturn the plans of the faithless and to undermine the hope that many have placed in false idols. Just as nothing can diminish God's faithfulness to His people, there is no way to work against God and prevail in the end.

PRAYER

Lord, Your plans cannot be overturned and Your power is without competitor. You are faithful to Your people and guide them to wholeness and life. May we follow Your paths and trust in the light of Your wisdom in our lives as we tell others of Your faithfulness. Amen.

41. GOD GUARDS YOU FROM DECEPTIVE THOUGHTS

Casting down imaginations, and every high thing that exalteth itself against the knowledge of God, and bringing into captivity every thought to the obedience of Christ. . .
2 CORINTHIANS 10:5

Paul wrote to the divided and disorderly church in Corinth that his personal actions would match his weighty letters, in which he used his authority to help build them up. While Paul's speeches were considered boring and his presence unimpressive, the God who inspired him to write would also guide him in his actions. The Spirit who guided him to write with power had granted him power to wage spiritual warfare against unseen strongholds and every deceptive thought that stood against the purposes and plans of God. Even if the Corinthian church had little fear of Paul based on his physical appearance or his speeches, they had every reason to be concerned about the ways God would punish their disobedience. Persisting in their rebellion against God and against His messenger had real consequences that they had not fully considered.

It's easy to make judgments of individuals

based on their outward appearance or manner of speaking. Paul challenges readers today to look deeper to the spiritual realities and the power of God behind those who preach, teach, disciple, evangelize, and minister. The power of the Spirit should not be underestimated when it comes to sharing the Gospel message, especially when encountering those who believe in falsehoods.

For those who lead, teach, or minister, God promises that their effectiveness in sharing His message isn't entirely up to them. They must rely on the Spirit's power in their lives, depending on God to destroy spiritual strongholds, arguments, and obstacles that may prevent them from reaching others. The wisdom and strength of man aren't enough to tear down these kinds of spiritual strongholds; they can be removed only through God's divine power.

PRAYER

Lord, You have given us Your divine power and wisdom to counter any arguments against Your purposes or any spiritual strongholds set up against You and Your people. May we rest in Your divine power today and find deliverance through Your intervention so that You gain all the glory for our work. Amen.

42. GOD GIVES YOU WISDOM

If any of you lack wisdom, let him ask of God, that giveth to all men liberally, and upbraideth not; and it shall be given him.
JAMES 1:5

God never promises His people that they will be spared from conflict or trials. Rather, Jesus promised that the Spirit would give them the words they required in the heat of the moment. James picked up on this theme, encouraging his readers to approach their trials with joy and even gratitude because trials would lead to a refined faith, a personal endurance, and a maturity in the ways of the Spirit that would strengthen them for the challenges that lay ahead. Throughout the suffering and trials that awaited them, James assured his readers that God would not only stay with them but generously provide wisdom for them.

There are plenty of reasons for Christians to doubt themselves, but those who trust completely in God's provision can take hope in the wisdom of God that is guaranteed to them. In fact, God's wisdom is promised to them as an abundant blessing. The one caveat is that only those who ask in faith will receive the blessing of God's wisdom. While doubt is something that must be faced honestly and worked through diligently, Christians seeking to receive direction and empowerment from God can't have a backup plan or expect God to fail them. Hard times will come, and doubts are always a real possibility for Christians who are stepping out in faith. However, those who seek God's wisdom should expect that God will come through, even if His deliverance or provision may not arrive in the expected way or on a preferred schedule.

PRAYER

Lord, You promise abundant wisdom to Your people and assure them that You will stand with them in their trials, guiding them to a stronger, more mature faith. Help us to stand in faith today as we look to You for wisdom and provision through our trials and uncertainties. Amen.

43. GOD REVEALS THE UNKNOWN TO YOU

*Call unto me, and I will answer thee,
and show thee great and mighty
things, which thou knowest not.*
JEREMIAH 33:3

While sitting as a prisoner among the court of the guard, waiting for the Chaldean army to overthrow the defensive fortifications of Jerusalem, Jeremiah heard God speak of the city's coming collapse and eventual restoration under the Lord. While the people around him worked to defend their city against siege ramps, Jeremiah was hated and imprisoned for sharing the message that their efforts were in vain. The city would be full of dead bodies after the walls fell. This was hardly the message anyone wanted to hear. Even more incredible, Jeremiah predicted that God would forgive the people of Israel for their sins, that Jerusalem would be rebuilt, and that the city would become a haven of prosperity and security. However, accepting this good news about the future required accepting the bad news of the present.

The story of Jeremiah and this passage in

particular shows the tension of God's revelation. Oftentimes, bad news goes along with the good news. The people of God may have to let go of their plans in the present. They may need to repent of sins and grievous failures. They may not be able to hold on to what they have built or what they hope to gain in the future.

On the other hand, God reveals a future beyond anyone's greatest hopes. Just as no one standing at the walls of Jerusalem could imagine a future of peace and prosperity, so do many Christians struggle to imagine God's blessings and restoration in their own lives. Those who seek the Lord may discover promises that stretch their faith and surpass their expectations.

PRAYER

Lord, You hold Your people accountable for their sins while also promising them blessings and restoration because of Your faithful love. May we entrust our unknown futures to You. As we face moments of despair, may we believe that You can guide us through the worst that life can bring. Amen.

44. GOD IS WITH YOU
WHEREVER YOU GO

Lo, I am with you always,
even unto the end of the world.
MATTHEW 28:20

The disciples had relied on Jesus to guide them and to teach them about God the Father. They frequently misunderstood His teachings and ran away in the Garden of Gethsemane when Jesus was in danger. Any observer would conclude that they had struggled to catch on to Jesus' ministry, even if they had enjoyed some success in preaching and casting out demons. With the prospect of Jesus leaving them on their own, they received a series of assurances for their mission: Jesus had all power and authority.

Jesus expected them to continue His ministry, making disciples, baptizing new believers, and teaching everyone to obey His commands. This mission was demanding, if not impossible, for mere people. They would require the intervention of Jesus Himself.

Believers today can step forward into ministry with this promise that Jesus goes with them. Whether they take the message of Jesus down the block or journey to the ends of the earth, they are assured Jesus will remain with them. This wasn't a onetime promise. This was an enduring promise that Christians can bank on until the end of time. Jesus will not abandon His people. His desire to reach all people even unto the ends of the earth remains, and so He will continue to guide His disciples who keep His ministry alive.

The authority and power of Jesus over everything in heaven and on earth remain potent and effective. How many Christians avail themselves of this promise as they begin their days?

PRAYER

Jesus, You promised Your disciples that You would remain with them and guide them for all of eternity, sharing Your power and authority with them as they completed Your work. May we trust fully in Your power and influence today so that we can share Your message with others in boldness and fidelity to Your ministry. Amen.

45. GOD REVEALS HIS HIDDEN DEPTHS TO YOU

But God hath revealed them unto us by his Spirit: for the Spirit searcheth all things, yea, the deep things of God.
1 CORINTHIANS 2:10

When Paul wrote about the wisdom and power that God granted to him, he challenged the faith and expectations of his readers in Corinth. They consistently doubted Paul, questioning whether his message was too good to be true. In addition, the Christians reading his letters were surrounded by people who second-guessed the wisdom of God. It wasn't just fantastic to teach that God was dwelling within His people; it was unbelievable to suggest that this same God had dwelled among people, died, and rose from the dead. This kind of hope had no equivalent, and so Paul tried to convince his readers that God's wisdom was far above whatever they could imagine.

For Christians today reading these words, Paul issues a challenge to trust in the wisdom and power of God, as well as in their inheritance of the Spirit. The teachings that Paul shared were not incongruous. He believed that every

Christian has access to the Spirit of God. As Christians seek to understand the depths of God's wisdom and mercy, they too have access to the Spirit. God desires to dwell among His people, to turn their hearts of stone into hearts of flesh, and to share His wisdom with them.

Paul promises a wisdom that comes not from human ideas but through God's power. The Spirit dwelling within believers enables them to understand the plans of God, the direction of scripture, and the will of God for His holy people.

PRAYER

Father, You have granted Your Holy Spirit to Your people and promise them wisdom and access to Your hidden depths. May we learn to wait on You, trust in Your Spirit's presence, and rely on the wisdom and knowledge that You grant us in Your mercy. Amen.

PROMISES OF PROTECTION

46. GOD'S NAME IS A STRONG TOWER

The name of the LORD is a strong tower:
the righteous runneth into it, and is safe.
PROVERBS 18:10

Proverbs contrasts two types of people. First, there are the rich who build up their wealth as if it's a strong city wall that can protect them from all calamities and threats. They are proud and self-reliant, trusting in their own power and resources to the point that they are haughty and destined for destruction.

Second, there are the righteous who recognize that their safety comes from the Lord Himself. They call on the Lord's name for their protection and deliverance. Much like a strong tower provides a greater chance of defeating an invader, the Lord stands as a certain help in time of need, never abandoning those who live in obedience and humility before Him.

Today there are many competing strong towers, from wealth, to influence, to personal wisdom and planning. Each of these strong towers attempts to make God irrelevant. They promise safety, but there is no guarantee they can deliver what they promise. Christians today have the guarantee of God's Spirit dwelling in them and of Christ as the Lord of all. He is the one true Strong Tower.

Calling on the name of the Lord today may be an unspectacular prayer of "Help!" or a more detailed request for help. Jesus assures His followers that whatever they ask in His name without doubting will be granted to them. When God's people pray with complete surrender and with eyes of faith looking up to God alone, they will find the safety and security promised in Proverbs.

PRAYER

Lord, You promise to deliver the righteous who trust You in times of need and uncertainty. May we turn away from every false source of hope that keeps us from trusting in You so that we can fully rely on the power of Your name to deliver us. May we give You the praise and glory You are due. Amen.

47. GOD IS YOUR SHIELD

But thou, O LORD, art a shield for me;
my glory, and the lifter up of mine head.
PSALM 3:3

The writer of this psalm had no shortage of enemies or reasons to despair. As enemies arose and doubters declared the limits of God's power, the psalmist had to come to a decision about trusting in God. How would he face the challenges around him and answer those who opposed him?

Rather than giving in to despair, the psalmist imagines God as an all-encompassing shield that protects him on all sides. There is no threat that God cannot guard against. While the resources of man may shield from the attacks on one side, there is nothing that God cannot see. God is worthy of his complete trust. The Lord lifts up his head in honor because he has chosen to trust completely in God.

God's people routinely face tough decisions about who they will trust and where they will seek honor. Perhaps there are sources of praise or adulation that Christians today view as competitors for the glory and honor that come from God alone. While trusting completely in the protection God provides may seem foolish or even cause some to view Christians with derision, God will surely see the faith of those who trust in Him and reward them richly. In addition to the promise of God's response and deliverance, those who trust in God alone as their shield will find rest. Even if their enemies multiply, the faithfulness of God today provides assurance for God's people that He will guard them in the future.

PRAYER

Lord, You hear the cries of Your people and promise to stand by them as their enemies taunt them and multiply. Increase our faith as we surrender our concerns and fears to You. May Your peace come to us as we rest in You. Amen.

48. GOD IS YOUR REFUGE

Trust in him at all times; ye people, pour out
your heart before him: God is a refuge for us.
PSALM 62:8

Two specific aspects of prayer are described in this psalm, and both are essential for a spirit of surrender and trust as God's people enter into prayer. Those who see God as their refuge learn to wait on God in silence, placing their hope in Him alone rather than in their own wisdom, resources, or relationships. It may be jarring to wait in silence, taking refuge in God alone. This disconnection from their words reminds God's people that their own wisdom won't deliver them. However, a time of silence before God may also stir up the very issues to bring before God in prayer. Oftentimes outward silence is coupled with an active mind where fears, worries, distractions, or sources of shame bubble to the surface.

Faced with the many worries of the heart, the psalmist advises God's people to pour out these matters to God. Only God, our trustworthy refuge, is strong enough to endure the waves of conflict that roll through life. Regardless of the circumstance, the people of

God have the same recourse: pouring out their hearts to God and taking refuge in Him.

Trusting in God is an "all or nothing" matter. Either God is a trustworthy rock in every circumstance, or God is as weak and inadequate as every other source of comfort and refuge in the world. The integrity of God's people is completely wrapped up in this total surrender to God. As God's people pour out their hearts to Him and wait in silence for His direction, they are assured that God alone will be honored in the end.

PRAYER

Father, may we turn to You in complete trust and childlike faith today, opening our hearts to share our hopes, fears, and disappointments and then waiting in silent anticipation. Our hope comes from You alone as we trust You to be our only refuge in life. Amen.

49. GOD DELIVERS
YOU FROM TROUBLES

*And the Lord shall deliver me from
every evil work, and will preserve me
unto his heavenly kingdom: to whom
be glory for ever and ever. Amen.*
2 TIMOTHY 4:18

In a time of extreme pressure, uncertainty, and danger, Paul found himself alone without anyone to stand by him or support him. In that moment of desperation and peril, the Lord faithfully stood by his side and reassured him that He would be present throughout every evil attack and safely bring him to His kingdom. That certainly didn't guarantee smooth sailing for the rest of his ministry, but Paul could face evil knowing that ultimately he belonged to the Lord and would one day rest by God's side in His heavenly kingdom. God would ensure that Paul would finish the ministry set in front of him before calling him to his heavenly home.

As Christians face trials, loss, or uncertainty today, these words of Paul provide reassurance that even during the hardest times and greatest dangers, God will not abandon His people. While Christians rightly desire to be surrounded by friends, family, and pastoral support in their darkest hours, God's comforting presence remains even if every other measure of support fails. Most importantly, God's promise of life and restoration in His kingdom offers Christians a source of hope and comfort as they face their final days on earth.

Christians can have such a sense of purpose and protection that they can step into danger with the hope that God will preserve them until they have finished His work. And when they breathe their final breath, they can rest knowing that they have been faithful to God's plans and will be rewarded one day.

PRAYER

Jesus, You have promised to stand by us in our moments of suffering and loss, providing strength to finish our journey here on earth and the comfort of Your presence as we pass to our heavenly home. May we boldly step forward in faith to where You have called us. Amen.

50. GOD PROTECTS YOU FROM DANGER

*But the Lord is faithful, who shall
stablish you, and keep you from evil.*
2 THESSALONIANS 3:3

Even though Paul was confident in God's power and calling for his ministry, he still knew he needed the prayer support of the church around him. In addition, they all needed the ongoing strength of God to prevail over those who wished to do them harm. Serving God and remaining true to the teachings of the Gospel didn't mean prosperity and safety for Paul and his fellow believers. If anything, their commitment to Jesus as their Lord and Savior put them directly at odds with civil and religious leaders as well as their neighbors. At times their lives were in danger, and they stood to lose their property or freedom at any moment.

Christians today face the same opposition from the forces of evil. While spiritual warfare today may not look quite as dramatic for many Christians when compared to what Paul and the Thessalonians endured, Christians should still expect opposition, if not outright attacks.

The evil that Christians face may be subtler and less dramatic, but the result could still be quite serious if Christians lose sight of their love for God.

Despite the challenges before Christians, God is faithful and can be trusted to guard and protect His people from evil. Christians today can share Paul's confidence that God's Spirit is at work in their lives and that Jesus has been granted all power and authority in heaven and on earth. God is not in a reactionary position but is actively defending His people from the dangers of this world.

PRAYER

Father, You are faithful to Your people and all-powerful to protect them from the evils and dangers that lurk in our world. Just as Paul and the early church trusted in Your power to deliver them from every harm, we trust You now to guide and direct us today so that we may be delivered and brought safely home to Your side one day. Amen.

51. GOD PROVIDES A WAY OUT WHEN YOU ARE TEMPTED

There hath no temptation taken you but such as is common to man: but God is faithful, who will not suffer you to be tempted above that ye are able; but will with the temptation also make a way to escape, that ye may be able to bear it.
1 CORINTHIANS 10:13

The temptations that God's people have faced throughout history are nothing new. The Bible tells stories of people who abandoned God, gave in to sexual temptation, complained against God, and opened themselves up to deception. These stories are reminders of the stakes of obedience and disobedience. The people of Israel faced these common challenges and temptations, and some endured significant losses. The people of God have a history of struggling with common temptations, so anyone who is proud or confident in their own strength or willpower should look to God instead for their help. God not only faithfully stands by His people but also guards them from being tested beyond their limits.

Whether Christians today believe their temptations are too much for them or they are strong enough on their own, Paul brings both viewpoints down to earth. No one should face temptations without God's support. Today's trial that appears to have no end may suddenly have a resolution that comes out of nowhere. A no-win situation may reach an unexpected outcome that honors all sides involved. When a temptation becomes too much to bear, those who call on the Lord for help will find strength and wisdom they didn't realize they had.

Facing temptation isn't a sin, but giving in to it is, and God is prepared to guide His people past it. Each test is an opportunity to remember the highs and lows of God's people in scripture and to seek God's provision of strength to endure and a way out when all appears lost.

PRAYER

Father, You have promised to help Your people stand up under their daily struggles with temptation and provide deliverance so that they can remain faithful. May we turn to You for wisdom and strength as we remember the generations before us who have passed through these same struggles. Amen.

52. GOD'S ANGELS PROTECT YOU

For he shall give his angels charge over
thee, to keep thee in all thy ways.
PSALM 91:11

The Psalms contrast the fate of the righteous and the unrighteous frequently, as the former trust God with their daily needs while the unrighteous look out for themselves, even to the detriment of others. Those who rebel against God are at the mercy of the dangers of this world and have no guarantee of one day entering the rest and peace of God's kingdom. While God's people are not promised complete safety from every manner of calamity, they have the assurance of God's presence and support throughout their lives. Angels stand by them to keep them secure in God.

In addition to God's faithfulness, those who trust in God as their only refuge have the promise of His angels walking with them throughout their days. Each moment is guarded by the angels of the Lord, ensuring that the followers of the Lord reach God's chosen purpose for them.

The Psalms are filled with laments that the wicked prosper and enjoy peace and safety while the people of God suffer. This psalm offers a different perspective, looking ahead to the fate of the wicked who leave God's protection behind and live according to their own desires and wisdom. They don't have the guarantee that God will carry them and guard them. Their choices will eventually catch up with them. But those who remain faithful to the Lord will pass through danger and conflict with security and will one day enter into God's rest.

PRAYER

Father, You have sent Your angels to guard and guide Your people through the trials and challenges of life. May we learn to rest in You each day, trusting in You as our secure rock and drawing comfort from the presence of Your angels who remain with us throughout each day. Amen.

53. YOU CAN KNOW GOD IS WITH YOU

Fear thou not; for I am with thee: be not dismayed; for I am thy God: I will strengthen thee; yea, I will help thee; yea, I will uphold thee with the right hand of my righteousness.
ISAIAH 41:10

The purposes and plans of God cannot be undermined by the power of men. Just as God called out Abraham as His own chosen servant and protected him from warring kings and powerful rulers, so God is able to guide and protect His people today. God stands by His people, strengthening them for the challenges of their lives and finishing the good works He began in them. Those who trust in God will see Him work to deliver them when they face opposition and trials.

Today God's people face uncertainty, conflict, and fearful situations. Many ministries may be in a position of instability or discouragement as they attempt to find a way forward. However, the Lord promises to strengthen them and uphold them. The Lord goes with the faithful people of God, never abandoning them when times become difficult.

Perhaps God's people struggle the most with discouragement when they forget that they have been chosen by God to be a light in the world and that God goes with them. When God's people feel alone or abandoned, they have forgotten that God has made covenants with His people for generations and has never abandoned them, even when they have been unfaithful. If the history of God's people is filled with examples of people forgetting their special place before God, the story of God is one of ongoing faithfulness and strength on behalf of His beloved people. The hope of God's people today is in the faithfulness of God and their calling to accomplish His purposes.

PRAYER

Father, You are faithful to generations of those who have been called to Your purpose. You have shown love and patience to those who abandoned You and returned with repentant hearts. May we remember that You remain with us today, showing us Your power and faithfulness throughout each day. Amen.

54. GOD GIVES YOU VICTORY OVER ENEMIES

When I cry unto thee, then shall mine enemies turn back: this I know; for God is for me.
PSALM 56:9

The Psalms frequently recount the tension of facing enemies who appear to be successful or on the brink of winning. Many times, the psalm writers wondered why it appeared that God had allowed the wicked to prosper while God's people suffered. However, these moments of confusion and even indignation often turned into a make-or-break moment of faith for God's people. Whom would God's people trust when it appeared that the enemy was close to winning?

In the highs and lows of spiritual life today, discouraging moments and personal sins can pile up. It may appear that those who ignore the commands of God have everything they need. However, when God's people turn to the Lord in faith, they will see that God is for them. These moments of testing often serve to reveal whom they have trusted in. Those who rely on their own wisdom will meet with frustration and loss, while those who call on the Lord will find Him more than able to stand by them.

Confidence grows from trusting in the Lord and seeing God's deliverance time and time again. This faith builds up over time so that God's people can praise the Lord in times of plenty and times of lack. What can men do to undermine the plans of God? Those who remain centered in God's will can stand on this solid ground and trust that God will finish His good work in them.

PRAYER

Lord, You desire for Your people to trust completely in You and Your divine power. May we learn to see that You are faithful and reliable when life becomes difficult. May we discover the peace and assurance that come from living each day in communion with Your will. Amen.

55. GOD GIVES YOU POWER OVER THE DEVIL

Put on the whole armour of God, that ye may be able to stand against the wiles of the devil.
EPHESIANS 6:11

What does it look like to stand strong in the Lord and in His power? Paul compared this to wearing armor, intentionally preparing for a struggle against the forces of evil in this world. This armor comes directly from God and is essential for anyone who hopes to stand firm in a time of testing and spiritual conflict.

Christians today have been given access to the strength of God through the indwelling Holy Spirit, and this gift of the Spirit is not just a source of comfort and reassurance. The Holy Spirit gives Christians access to the full armor of God in their lives. By seeking God's presence and the Spirit's intervention each day, they can stand up against the power of the devil. Failure to seek the Spirit of God is a failure to see what's really at work around Christians each day. Without God's guidance and the Spirit's empowerment, they are preparing to be blindsided.

A confrontation with spiritual forces requires a spiritual defense. God offers His people the resources of faith, the Word of God, and the assurance of salvation to guard them as they face the spiritual dangers of each day. By praying in the Spirit regularly, they will remain in touch with the Spirit and equipped with God's power. It's a mistake to focus only on earthly struggles and adversaries that can be seen. The spiritual forces in the world are poised to strike God's people, and only those living in the power of the Spirit will be prepared for the spiritual fight that is sure to come.

PRAYER

Father, You have generously given Your people access to Your holy Spirit and promise that You will equip them with armor for the spiritual battles that could upend their faith. May we find space throughout today to pray in the Spirit, and may the protective words of scripture take hold in our lives. Amen.

56. GOD GIVES YOU AUTHORITY OVER SATAN

And the God of peace shall bruise Satan under your feet shortly. The grace of our Lord Jesus Christ be with you. Amen.
ROMANS 16:20

The spiritual battles that the people of Rome faced each day extended throughout the church and into their personal relationships. At times, the conflict may have seemed endless. Would they ever enter into the peace of God? Paul assured them that Satan's days of causing discouragement, unbelief, and divisions were numbered. God would soon bring peace and harmony to His people by crushing Satan. In fact, the people of God would see Satan crushed under their feet just as God promised to do to the serpent. The people empowered by the living Christ would be involved in the completion of God's redemptive work.

Christians today can trust that their spiritual struggles will not go on forever. There will come a day when Satan will be crushed under their feet because of Jesus Christ's victory. The obedience of God's people is not in vain, since God will reward them richly for their faithfulness, while those who serve their own appetites and work toward their own ambitions will find themselves cut off from God.

When God's people finally have ultimate victory over Satan, they will experience the full extent of God's grace that is already with them. For now, God will continue to empower His people so that they can live with wisdom, avoid evil, and overcome the temptations of this life. The promises of God remain today, even if they are not yet fully realized. The Spirit is a guarantee that God will one day bring this victory to its completion.

PRAYER

Lord, You have conquered the powers of darkness and promised us that we will one day crush Satan under our feet. May we live with an awareness of the powers of darkness around us and live in obedience to You as we trust in Your power to deliver us today and to complete Your victory in the days to come. Amen.

PROMISES OF RELATIONSHIP

57. GOD GIVES YOU YOUR HEART'S DESIRES

Delight thyself also in the LORD: and he shall give thee the desires of thine heart.
PSALM 37:4

Obedience to the Lord is a long-term hope for the people of God as they commit their plans to God and wait on Him to fulfill His promises and bring about their deliverance. In the short term, it may appear that the wicked have prospered and the worst of the wrong-doers have gained every advantage. From God's perspective, however, their plans for domination and security are about as long-lasting as the grass that fades in the scorching sun. Any gains will burn up as surely as a fragile plant.

The way of God is the path to security and long-lasting hope. But trusting in the Lord doesn't just result in security for the long term. Rather than relying on their own plans, their personal wisdom, or the expectations of those around them to guide their actions, God's people learn to surrender their future to God.

When God's people trust their ways to Him, they are in a position to delight in the Lord as they watch Him working in their lives and guiding their way forward.

Living by faith brings about a transformation in which God's people grow in their trust and take greater delight in the Lord. As the cloud of sin is removed from their lives, they are able to discern the desires of their hearts and see how God can bring those desires to fruition. While wrongdoers watch their accomplishments fall apart, those who trust in the Lord have the promise that God will act on their behalf and lead them even to unexpected blessings.

PRAYER

Lord, You delight in Your people and desire that they delight in You, promising to grant them the desires of their hearts. May we live in faith and commitment to You and Your ways so that we may enjoy Your blessings and experience the renewal of our hearts and minds. Amen.

58. GOD BLESSES YOUR MARRIAGE

So God created man in his own image,
in the image of God created he him; male
and female created he them. And God blessed
them, and God said unto them, Be fruitful, and
multiply, and replenish the earth, and subdue it:
and have dominion over the fish of the sea,
and over the fowl of the air, and over every
living thing that moveth upon the earth.
GENESIS 1:27–28

Marriage is a blessing from God that models the complete image of God. When a man and woman are joined together, they reflect the image of the Creator: "In the image of God created he him; male and female created he them." Most importantly, as a reflection of God's image in creation, the man and woman were joined together not only in their identity but in their vocation to care for God's creation and to fill the earth with people.

While single people are created in God's image and reflect God whether or not they ever marry, the blessing of marriage is one opportunity to reflect God's desire for love and companionship. Marriage becomes a way that people can partner together to care for creation with the support of another. This blessed union reflects the unity and joint purpose of the Trinity with its love and lifelong commitment. Marriage becomes a way for humans to tell the rest of creation about who God is and what God values.

Those who are married have an opportunity today to ask for God's blessing and guidance in their marriage. The call of married couples to support one another, to be fruitful and multiply, and to care for the rest of the world requires them to depend on God's help to remain committed to each other for the rest of their lives. Thankfully, God is deeply invested in preserving marriages and ensuring that they have a life-giving, redemptive impact in His world.

PRAYER

Lord, You have created men and women to reflect Your love and to care for Your creation. May we experience Your help to either live in faithfulness and commitment in our own marriages or to support the married couples in our communities. May we reflect Your commitment to these marriage partnerships. Amen.

59. GOD BLESSES FAMILIES
WITH CHILDREN

Lo, children are an heritage of the LORD:
and the fruit of the womb is his reward.
As arrows are in the hand of a mighty
man; so are children of the youth.
PSALM 127:3–4

Children were essential for any functioning family in the time of ancient Israel. Without children, especially male descendants, families lacked a line of succession to take over the inheritance, including keeping the family land in place. Families saw children as the ones who would continue their name and keep their family traditions alive for years to come. Children were also essential for working the land, keeping family businesses sustainable, and caring for their parents in their old age. Families could expect very real long-term economic hardships without direct descendants, and this reality often put pressure on married couples to have children as soon as possible.

While the stories of scripture that involve infertile couples make it clear that families without children are not being punished by God, they do help drive home the truth that many families see their children as blessings from God. Children can change the dynamics of a family and even add some complications at times, yet they are undoubtedly a sign of God's presence and blessing in a family. Just as a warrior saw his arrows as a sign of strength and preparation, so can families see their children as a strength to be cherished.

Children continue the work of God for future generations, passing the teachings and blessings of God from one generation to the next. As God acts on behalf of His people, He hopes they will pass stories of His mercy and blessings on to future generations, giving families a heritage of holiness and faithfulness.

PRAYER

Father, You care for Your people by giving them children as blessings for generations to come. May we care for our children, protect them, and ensure that they are aware of Your power and mercy so that they will pass along a God-fearing heritage for years to come. Amen.

60. GOD GIVES YOU FRIENDS AND FAMILY

God setteth the solitary in families:
he bringeth out those which are bound with
chains: but the rebellious dwell in a dry land.
PSALM 68:6

God is particularly concerned about those who are isolated or lack the support of friends and family. God sees the orphans and widows who have no immediate support network to protect them in their times of great need. God cares for the desolate who lack a home to live in or any measure of long-term security or shelter. Even prisoners who have lost so much and face an uncertain future with their damaged reputations and limited resources are of deep concern to God as they seek to reenter society and take their next steps.

Today, God is inviting His people to take notice of those who are vulnerable, who lack resources, who are cut off from support networks, or who remain isolated from their communities—for example, a widow or orphan, a newly released prisoner, or someone living in a home without any connection to family or neighbors. Nursing homes and hospice houses may be places of particularly great need. Regardless of the circumstances, God desires that desolate and solitary people are blessed with families and communities. He wants to see those who have failed in the past pursue a redemptive and restorative path. Oftentimes relationship networks are what separate the financially struggling from poverty.

Those who enjoy prosperity and material blessings have a great deal to share with others. Perhaps the best benefit of this prosperity is the opportunity to share it with those who have no other source of support or comfort. Those who enjoy the connections of friends and families can share these communities with those who are alone.

PRAYER

Father, You see the people in need throughout our communities and desire to meet their needs for food, shelter, family members, and friendships. May we share generously from our time and resources with others so that they may experience the blessings You desire for them today. Amen.

61. GOD GIVES YOU A GOOD REPUTATION

Having Your conversation honest among the Gentiles: that, whereas they speak against you as evildoers, they may by Your good works, which they shall behold, glorify God in the day of visitation.
1 PETER 2:12

Christians live as exiles in this world as God's chosen children who have been called to conduct their lives according to God's commands. The conduct of Christians may appear honorable before God as they seek to follow the teachings of the Bible, but among those who don't share their values or morals, these Christians may appear foolish or even suspicious in their words and deeds. The Christian life never aims to win the approval of other people, especially those outside the faith, but unfamiliarity with the ways of God can cause problems and misunderstandings that prompt non-Christians to slander the reputation of Christians.

Such a possibility does not deter Peter, and Christians today should heed his advice. Peter counsels believers to live honorably and righteously, obeying God's commands rather than yielding to the expectations and cultural norms of the times. Regardless of what is said about Christians, they have only one God to serve and there will be only one judge over humanity at the end of time.

This single-minded focus on pleasing God and obeying His commands puts the reputation of Christians firmly in the hands of God. Only God can exonerate those who are written off by the rest of the world as "evildoers" or dishonorable people. In the face of such charges, Christians can resolve to act honorably among the Gentiles without provoking them, remembering that their fate does not hinge on winning the praise of those who reject the wisdom of God.

PRAYER

Father, I thank You that we belong to You and Your heavenly kingdom, where You will judge all in righteousness, seeing our deeds for what they are and rewarding our faithfulness. Grant us patience and mercy for those who misunderstand our calling as Your children so that we may glorify You today. Amen.

62. GOD LOOKS ON
YOU WITH FAVOR

*Blessed be the Lord God of Israel; for he
hath visited and redeemed his people.*
LUKE 1:68

The people of Israel had endured unfaithfulness, invasions, and military occupations. Their religious leaders were divided, and their people were unsure of how God could ever lead them toward redemption under the powerful rule of Rome. As Zechariah considered the ministry of his son John and the coming savior from the house of Jacob, he saw that while many had tried to follow the law perfectly in order to prompt God to send the Messiah to save Israel, it was only God's covenant love for His people that brought about this great moment of salvation.

The ministry of Jesus ushered in a time of God's favor that has been extended to all who are willing to accept His message. While there are plenty of ways to reject the favor of God, there is no way to "earn" it. The covenant love of God had been given generously from one generation to another with the promise that God would one day visit His people to save them. In this time of unprecedented favor, Jesus welcomed all who would believe His message and follow His teachings.

Christians today partake in this same favor from God. There is nothing anyone can do to win God's favor. It has been given freely as a gift, but it can be neglected or obscured by disobedience, busyness, selfish ambition, and so on. The message of Zechariah remains true today: God has come down and visited His people to redeem them. God has come to show His favor today, but how will God's people respond when they hear His voice?

PRAYER

Gracious Lord, You have chosen to redeem Your people because it is Your good pleasure to show Your favor and to make Your salvation available based on grace. May we turn away from the sins and distractions that keep us from You so that we can fully experience Your redemption and share it with others. Amen.

63. GOD GIVES YOU ENCOURAGING WORDS

*If there be therefore any consolation in Christ,
if any comfort of love, if any fellowship of the
Spirit, if any bowels and mercies, fulfil ye my
joy, that ye be likeminded, having the same
love, being of one accord, of one mind.*
PHILIPPIANS 2:1–2

When Christians are brought together into the same family under Christ, they are also brought into relationships that should be life giving and encouraging as they share the same mission and mind-set as Christ. The Philippian church in particular had its fair share of challenges after seeing Paul imprisoned, released by an earthquake in the night, and then virtually chased out of town. The leaders of the town opposed the message that Paul passed on to them, making the church's future uncertain, if not dangerous. The source of their comfort and hope in this time was their commitment to mutual encouragement because of their bonds in Christ.

Christians today share in the same Spirit and have been joined to the same family in Christ. Nothing has changed in that regard from the time of Paul. While there will always be room for personal differences as well as strengths and weaknesses, the sign that the church is living under the influence of the Spirit is its commitment to loving one another, sharing the same goals, and encouraging one another in Christ.

Paul held up Jesus as a model of laying down His own interests and viewing Himself with humility as He came down to earth. Much like their crucified Lord, the Philippians would find greater unity and encouragement by placing their own preferences and priorities behind those of their fellow believers. There is no place in a unified church for selfish ambition and pride, as these will tear apart the bonds that unite the church. Unity happens when Christians learn to view others as better than themselves.

PRAYER

Jesus, You came to earth in humility and service to humanity, not flaunting Your divine power or demanding the honor and respect that rightly belonged to You. Help us to imitate Your example, leaving our own preferences behind, supporting those who need encouragement, and living a life of humility and love. Amen.

64. GOD GIVES YOU WISE ADVICE TO SHARE

*And God gave Solomon wisdom
and understanding exceeding much,
and largeness of heart, even as the
sand that is on the sea shore.*
1 KINGS 4:29

God didn't grant Solomon wisdom be-cause God only cares about kings. While Solomon had a particularly great responsibility to lead the people of God, he received wisdom from God because he saw his great need for God's help. The special thing about Solomon's request was the humility that preceded it. He saw the massive responsibility before him of leading Israel, and he knew that he would re-quire God's help in order to serve others well. How else could he faithfully serve in the posi-tion God had given him? This humble request placed his life in God's hands. If he achieved anything great in his role as king of Israel, it would be traced back to the power of God in his life.

As God's people consider what they are called by God to do or as they view opportuni-ties for ministry, a foundational starting point is their great need for God's intervention. The work of God is a calling that will exhaust human resources, but those who trust in God will find wisdom and strength beyond their expectations. The difference isn't how qualified or capable people are to fulfill God's calling, but rather how greatly they are willing to depend on God.

Solomon's request for wisdom is an opportunity for Christians today to step back from their challenges and humbly ask for God's intervention and direction. God desires to help His people, especially when they seek to share His wisdom and blessings with others. The wisdom of God is not given for personal benefit but for the building up of others so that they learn of God's greatness.

PRAYER

Lord, You generously grant wisdom to those who humble themselves before You and ask for Your aid. As we seek to serve and minister to others this week, give us wisdom and understanding so that we can share Your goodness freely and meet every challenge that comes before us. Amen.

65. GOD HELPS YOU
DENY YOURSELF

I am crucified with Christ: nevertheless I live; yet not I, but Christ liveth in me: and the life which I now live in the flesh I live by the faith of the Son of God, who loved me, and gave himself for me.
GALATIANS 2:20

Christians who try to imitate Christ on their own are destined for failure and frustration. Paul's picture of the Christian life is a striking challenge: he considers that his old self has been crucified with Christ so that holy living on his part must come from God alone, not from his own efforts. The old man has been removed and the life of God is what animates and guides him. This means his sins have also been crucified with Christ, and he stands forgiven and redeemed, perfect before God because he has been united with the life of Christ. Each day for Paul was an act of faith because he relied on the life of Christ to empower him.

Holy living today is so much more than choice or willpower for Christians. Rather, it comes down to identity. Those who are loved by God and have taken part in the death and resurrection of Christ have a new identity in the risen Lord that enables them to live in holiness. While Christians can ignore their identity in Christ or choose to turn away from God, their new lives come through the loving sacrifice of Christ.

Each day for the Christian is an opportunity to live by faith in the Son of God. The Christian life comes from Christ, not from the rules that Christians set up for themselves. Rather than condemning people for their sins, Jesus suffered and gave His life to free His people from sin and impart His redemptive power to them.

PRAYER

Jesus, You offered Yourself in love and compassion for those who were disobedient and in need of Your mercy so they could be transformed. May we count our old selves as dead so that we can live in complete dependence on You and experience the power of Your present life to redeem us. Amen.

PROMISES OF PROVISION

66. GOD SUPPLIES ALL YOUR NEEDS

But my God shall supply all your need according to his riches in glory by Christ Jesus.
PHILIPPIANS 4:19

When Paul was in need, he always knew he could count on the Philippian church to give generously to his ministry. Over time, he saw that their generosity to his ministry, even if it meant great hardship to them, had become a pleasing sacrifice to God. As they recognized the value of Paul's work and gave generously, they gained God's attention as if they had burned a pleasing sacrifice before Him. Rather than preserving their own security, they placed themselves in God's hands, trusting that God's work through Paul was more important than storing up treasure for themselves. Most importantly, Paul saw that God has unexhausted riches, both materially and spiritually, that He readily shares with those who place the kingdom of God first.

When God's people place the needs of others first, they can break the attachment to possessions and material markers of success that threatens to hold them back from God. In addition, those who freely share their resources and blessings with others will find a simple way to ensure that the kingdom of God remains a higher priority than their own security.

God is eager to care for the needs of His people, but materialism can become a snare for Christians. There is a difference between trusting in God's daily provision for one's needs and serving the priorities of wealth and financial security. Those who take care of God's kingdom work can trust that God will also take care of them. However, those who develop their own safety nets may soon find that they have no need for God's provision and care.

PRAYER

Lord, You desire to bless Your people and care for their needs by inspiring Your people to be generous with what they have. May we evade the traps of materialism and the temptation to serve money so that we can enjoy the freedom of Your provision each day and share our resources freely with others. Amen.

67. GOD BLESSES YOUR GENEROSITY

The LORD thy God shall bless thee in all thy works,
and in all that thou puttest thine hand unto.
DEUTERONOMY 15:10

Money is often one of the most challenging obstacles in the Christian life because it can easily take the place of God and lead to various corrupt practices. The love of money is even called the root of evil because of the ways it touches other moral decisions. While Christians are called to love God and their neighbors, earning money often gets in the way of acts of charity because earning money can place demands on time, managing money can cause anxiety, and spending money on possessions can lead to many distracting pursuits. In a culture that values wise investments and the careful accumulation of wealth, money can be an especially powerful barrier between neighbors.

When God gave the people of Israel the laws for their new nation, He mandated that they should be generous to those in need, lending to those who had needs even if the loan would never bring a significant return or even lead to financial loss. The challenge for God's people was to put the needs of their neighbors first rather than ensuring their own financial security. Such tight-fisted practices revealed that they were more concerned about protecting themselves and didn't trust in God's provision.

God promises the generous that He will take care of their needs just as they have taken care of the needs of their neighbors. They will enjoy success in their work and prosperity in their new endeavors. Anything that is lost in making loans to others will be recovered through what the Lord gives them in their new ventures. For those concerned about their financial future, generosity may be the next step forward.

PRAYER

Father, You desire that all people have their basic needs met so that they can flourish without fear of hunger or poverty. May we share our resources in faith with anyone who makes a request of us, trusting that our financial security rests completely in You and Your generosity toward us. Amen.

68. GOD BLESSES FAITHFULNESS AT WORK

*And let the beauty of the LORD our
God be upon us: and establish thou
the work of our hands upon us; yea,
the work of our hands establish thou it.*
PSALM 90:17

After years of toil and hardship, the people of Israel called out to God for compassion and mercy. They had seen evil for too long, and they yearned to experience God's loving kindness so that they could rejoice in it throughout their days. They saw that their future prosperity was entwined with the favor of the Lord, whether that came in the form of seasonal rains for their harvests or peace and stability in their country. They looked to the Lord expectantly for a time of favor and prosperity.

This simple prayer for God's beauty to rest on His people is one that God's people can continue to pray today. This is not a request for fame or riches, only for God's loving presence to make the most of His people's work each day. Those who ask God to establish their work are asking for stability and effectiveness as they set about their daily tasks. Rather than seeing a day's work come to nothing or adversaries undermine their work, Christians can ask God to be present with them throughout their days, guiding them and guarding them as they make decisions with integrity and work with focus and diligence.

God is glorified in the work that His people accomplish. Each workday is an opportunity for Christians to show their faith in God's provision and direction. The "how" of each workday matters to the Lord as much as "what" has been produced at the day's end. Those who carry out their work in faith, depending on God's support, will have all the more reason to praise God for His faithfulness.

PRAYER

All-powerful God, You are present with Your people in their daily tasks and the challenges they face at work, and You desire to show Your faithfulness by establishing the work of Your people. May we begin each workday with faith and trust in Your power and presence. Amen.

69. GOD MAKES YOU SUCCESSFUL

*This book of the law shall not depart out
of thy mouth; but thou shalt meditate therein
day and night, that thou mayest observe to
do according to all that is written therein:
for then thou shalt make thy way prosperous,
and then thou shalt have good success.*
JOSHUA 1:8

God's plan for success is strikingly simple. While Joshua had to contemplate military plans and settlement details in the Promised Land, he had a very simple instruction to take to heart: meditate on this book of the law day and night. By striving to live in faithful obedience to God, the people of Israel would remain focused on what was most important for their future. Their security, success, and prosperity meant nothing if they were not fully committed to the Lord and living in accordance with His commands.

The key for God's people to remain faithful and committed to the Lord's ways requires attentiveness and time, but remains simple today: meditate on the teachings of the Lord. Those who know what God expects of them and how they should conduct their lives will be far more likely to obey those teachings. As God's people regularly make time to meditate on scripture, they will find that it counteracts any negative influences in their lives. It may be said that people become what they meditate on.

Joshua's message makes the stakes clear for readers today: those who want to find success in life without obedience to God have the order of things backward. Obedience comes before every other priority, and even those who experience success may find that it is hollow if they fail to observe the commands of God. Without prioritizing obedience to God, they will gradually slip away from the Lord, make compromises, and even take actions that damage their reputations.

PRAYER

Lord, You call Your people to devote themselves to regular meditation on Your message and commands so that they can remain united with You and Your people. May we prioritize obedience to Your teachings over any accomplishment we can achieve today while never becoming servants to our success. Amen.

70. GOD MADE YOU UNIQUE

For we are his workmanship, created in Christ Jesus unto good works, which God hath before ordained that we should walk in them.
EPHESIANS 2:10

A person's calling can be difficult to determine when there are so many competing priorities and challenges in life. However, each Christian's primary calling is a life of good works according to the plans of God and through the power of Christ. Jesus saved His people by grace and now enables them to bless others. The even better news for those uncertain about their future is that God has prepared the course for His people to do these works.

A good question for Christians based on this passage could be: "What good works have I done today for others?" Jesus saves His people so they can continue His work on earth. The transformational power of Christ isn't limited to personal salvation. It enables Christians to seize the opportunities around them to serve others.

The Ephesian church found that it can be tempting to try to live well enough to earn God's favor, but Jesus taught that no one can earn God's favor. It is a grace freely given to God's people. Christians are created anew in God and even called His "workmanship" because they live through His power, not by their own wisdom or goodness. Christians today who live by God's power can then boast of the power of God in their lives rather than their own goodness. The snare of pride is removed and the faith of the church is strengthened so that its members learn to depend on God for all of their needs.

PRAYER

Jesus, You have saved Your people from sin and restored them by Your grace to live as Your new creation. May we live in gratitude and by faith in the new life that You grant us so that we can do the good works You have set before us. May we boast only of Your power at work in us. Amen.

71. GOD BLESSES YOU PERFECTLY

Every good gift and every perfect gift
is from above, and cometh down from
the Father of lights, with whom is no
variableness, neither shadow of turning.
JAMES 1:17

Many different worries can fill a day. From worries over finances to concerns over job security to anxiety about personal relationships, we can easily spend an entire day looking at what isn't going well or what could fall apart at any moment. However, God is consistent in His loving concern for His people, with no changes in His support, love, or commitment. It's understandable for people to worry, but worry misses out on what God desires for His people.

From material to spiritual blessings, God cares for His people perfectly, giving them what they need. That isn't to say they will never face difficult or uncertain times. Rather, a difficult time is an opportunity to turn to God in faith, trusting that God has the perfect spiritual, relational, or material gifts His people need. God's people have been called to fulfill His purpose and to reveal His loving-kindness to others. Christians can trust that they have not been abandoned but that God stands by them. In times of darkness, God sheds His light to show the way forward. In times of scarcity, God leads His people to the perfect blessing they need.

Through the blessings God shares with His people, they are able to reveal His goodness to others. Their testimonies of provision become one of the means God uses to reach others with His goodness. Rather than focusing on what isn't right yet, Christians can thank God for the good gifts they've already received, believing that God isn't done with them.

PRAYER

Father, You delight in providing for Your children, caring for their needs and blessing them abundantly so that they can testify to Your goodness and generosity. May we see the perfect gifts You have already given us so that we can trust You to provide for our needs in the days to come. Amen.

72. GOD BLESSES YOU WHEN YOU GIVE

Every man according as he purposeth in his heart, so let him give; not grudgingly, or of necessity: for God loveth a cheerful giver.
2 CORINTHIANS 9:7

When Paul sought to raise money for the Christians suffering in Jerusalem, he encouraged the Corinthian church to stop worrying about their own situation. Rather, they should focus on the joyful result of their giving that would meet the dire needs of their fellow believers. Their financial gifts would make a tremendous difference, and whatever they gave could be easily replaced by God as their own needs emerged. More importantly, their generosity would open them up to God's blessings as they participated in God's work and disconnected themselves from attachments to money. Generosity is a way to address the priorities of one's life, and it remains a vitally important part of the spiritual disciplines that Christians practice.

The way that Christians give matters, since God wants to address the heart's attachment to money and ensure that His people depend on Him, not on their finances. God wants donations to be made with joy rather than a sense of compulsion or obligation, because joyful givers recognize that money will not save them and that it's more important to help others than to shore up personal stability.

In addition, each person's financial resources are a gift from God stewarded only for a season. No one can take their wealth with them at the end of life, so generosity maintains a healthy perspective on wealth. Christians who cheerfully give to others are the most aware of God's power and provision as they trust that their actions make them righteous before God and serve the function of helping more people experience God's love and presence.

PRAYER

Father, You desire Your people to join in the freedom and joy of generous giving so that we will not be servants to our wealth or possessions. May we experience the joy of giving in faith as we participate in the work of Your kingdom by sharing our blessings with those in need. Amen.

73. GOD BLESSES ACCORDING TO YOUR GENEROSITY

Give, and it shall be given unto you; good measure, pressed down, and shaken together, and running over, shall men give into your bosom. For with the same measure that ye mete withal it shall be measured to you again.
LUKE 6:38

God opens others to become generous when they also experience generosity, and so Jesus' teachings on topics such as judgment and generosity challenged His followers to embody what they hoped to see in others. This isn't just a principle for leaders and those in authority. Jesus suggested that His followers could counteract the power abusers and tight-fisted mind-set of their time by actively becoming the change anyone would hope to see. Although there was no guarantee everyone would respond so graciously to their generosity, over time, His followers would see benefits come to them as more people imitated their generous giving.

As Christians today manage their finances, review organizations to support, and look for ways to be generous in their communities, they have the potential to unleash a significant movement of generosity, whether it be generosity of time, resources, or money. By generously giving to others, Christians can bring about a culture change where more people catch Jesus' vision of joyfully meeting the needs of others and trusting God to provide what they need when their own challenges arise. Giving is an opportunity for Christians to live by faith and to fully embrace the provision of God in their lives as they watch Him return their generosity through others.

PRAYER

Jesus, You have blessed us with resources that we can freely and joyfully share with others so that their needs are met and they too can participate in generosity to others. May we give out of faith and hope, knowing that You can supply our needs when we make our requests known to You. Amen.

74. GOD BLESSES YOU
WHEN YOU TITHE

*Bring ye all the tithes into the storehouse,
that there may be meat in mine house, and
prove me now herewith, saith the LORD of hosts,
if I will not open you the windows of heaven,
and pour you out a blessing, that there shall
not be room enough to receive it.*
MALACHI 3:10

The Israelites struggled with tithing a portion of their income toward the temple and the priests who served God, and the Lord spoke clearly through Malachi: they were robbing God! Of course, many of the people could explain their stingy giving by citing their need to have enough money on hand or fears about the security of their fields and orchards. They faced genuine concerns about meeting their most basic needs, and so they held back their tithes and offerings from God.

While God's people today can surely relate to this fear, the Lord's reply is a test of faith that was challenging back in Malachi's time and remains so in the present: give the full tithe and the Lord will provide an overflowing blessing. Some teachers today have exploited these passages in order to accumulate wealth or build larger facilities. This promise from God addressed the basic obedience of the people and had nothing to do with the grandeur of the temple itself. They had to take the commands of the Lord at face value and then live in faith that God would provide for them.

This is a powerful shift in thinking for believers that puts tithing as the first line item in every household budget. Get generosity right, and everything else will fall into place from there as God provides for His people. In addition to teaching God's people to live by faith, regular tithing also prevents believers from making money too high of a priority or spending too much on personal indulgences. Tithing helps keep the power of money in check as God's people set aside a portion of it for the Lord's use.

PRAYER

Lord, You generously provide for our needs and promise that if we place obedient giving ahead of our own concerns, You will bless us richly from Your abundance to the point that our blessings overflow. May we obediently give our full tithes to You this week and trust in Your provision for tomorrow. Amen.

75. GOD FREES YOU FROM WORRY

Therefore take no thought, saying, What shall we eat? or, What shall we drink? or, Wherewithal shall we be clothed? (For after all these things do the Gentiles seek:) for your heavenly Father knoweth that ye have need of all these things. But seek ye first the kingdom of God, and his righteousness; and all these things shall be added unto you.
MATTHEW 6:31–33

If every Christian made a list of their needs today, not a single item on it would surprise God. God is well aware of what His people need: food, clothing, shelter, and income. God also knows what His creation requires, providing sunlight, rain, and soil for the flowers of the fields, giving them what they need at the right time. God's people are so much more valuable than plants that wither in the scorching heat, and He desires His people to entrust their concerns about each day to Him so that they can see His power at work in their lives.

Concerns over financial safety and personal well-being are understandable, but they can also become an obsession. Some of the means to safety and stability can become distractions even from the pursuit of God, as Jesus noted that the Gentiles sought after these things. Looking out for one's own well-being can become an all-consuming quest that becomes the measuring stick of one's life. While the Father doesn't deny the urgency of basic needs for His people, He asks that they seek the higher goals of His kingdom, chasing after holiness and living in obedience to His commands.

By seeking the Lord and prioritizing righteous living, Christians will free themselves from the vain pursuit of fleeting security in this world. They will no longer live with their worries from one day to the next. Most importantly, they will find true stability in the promises of Christ while also seeing God meet all of their needs.

PRAYER

Jesus, You have reassured us that You care about meeting our needs and that our concerns will be taken care of if we put the kingdom of God first. Help us to lay down our worries and fears so that we can grow in faith and continue Your ministry. Amen.

76. GOD GIVES ACCORDING TO YOUR FAITH

He that is faithful in that which is least is faithful also in much: and he that is unjust in the least is unjust also in much. If therefore ye have not been faithful in the unrighteous mammon, who will commit to your trust the true riches?
LUKE 16:10–11

While it's tempting to believe that many of life's problems could be solved by more money, more influence, or more power, Jesus made a sobering statement that should cause Christians to pause and reconsider. Following a story of a shrewd manager who used his influence and wealth to win friends and to secure support after losing his position, Jesus commended the manager for wisely using his resources because he understood the stakes and how to plan for the long term.

Jesus wants His followers to understand their circumstances and to remember that God has entrusted them with resources and blessings that they can squander or use wisely. Most importantly, Christians have been entrusted with the message of eternal life, and this is the resource they cannot afford to misuse. Either they can serve God and work toward the purposes of the kingdom of God, or they can serve their own plans and fail to use their access to the kingdom for the benefit of others.

Christians can't hedge their bets by splitting time between serving God and serving money. This divided attention draws them away from the unparalleled calling of sharing the riches of eternal life with others. Either the Gospel is the most important message to share, or it isn't. No middle path can be forged here. While Jesus' use of an economics lesson to speak to the costs and rewards of discipleship may be jarring, the simplicity of comparing God's kingdom to actual riches challenges Christians to truly live by faith by pursuing the kingdom first.

PRAYER

Jesus, You call us to lives of holiness and devotion to the kingdom of God so that we can enjoy the fellowship You share with God and tell others about the new life You give. May we count the cost of discipleship and put the priorities of Your kingdom above every other goal this day. Amen.

77. GOD DOES MORE THAN YOU ASK FOR

*Now unto him that is able to do exceeding
abundantly above all that we ask or think,
according to the power that worketh in us.*
EPHESIANS 3:20

The church in Ephesus had good reasons to be discouraged and concerned about the future. Paul had been suffering greatly as he faithfully shared the Gospel message, and they faced significant opposition throughout their city. Following Jesus became even more hazardous when powerful craftsmen that feared losing their business making idols began to actively oppose the church. With so many enemies aligning against them, Paul directed them to place their faith in God the Father and trust that God could do more than they asked or imagined.

How much time do Christians spend worrying about the size of their problems compared to the amount of time they spend on their knees before God? It's true that this idea has become a cliché of sorts for many Christians, but for Paul, time in prayer was the testing ground of faith. Those who spend time on their knees before the Father will be strengthened in their inner being by the Holy Spirit and will become more aware of Christ dwelling in their hearts. Such grounding in the presence of God becomes essential for facing the highs and lows of the spiritual life.

Most importantly, those who spend time in prayer before the Father will gain an assurance of God's love for them, seeing its height, width, length, and depth with greater clarity. Those who pray with the confidence that they are loved by God will grow to expect more from the Father who will never abandon His children in their time of need.

PRAYER

Jesus, You have sent Your Spirit to dwell within us so that we may be strengthened and prepared for suffering and trials. May we kneel in prayer with confidence that we are loved beyond what we can imagine and that Your power in us can accomplish more than we could think to ask. Amen.

PROMISES OF ENCOURAGEMENT

78. GOD'S PLANS EXCEED YOUR OWN

For I know the thoughts that I think toward you, saith the LORD, thoughts of peace, and not of evil, to give you an expected end.
JEREMIAH 29:11

The exiled people of Judah had two messages to consider. On the one hand, they had prophets and diviners who promised the people that they would return to their own land in a short time. On the other hand, Jeremiah had a very different message, promising that the people *would* return to their land, but only after seventy years of exile. Jeremiah claimed to represent the only true message from God, but not surprisingly his message wasn't popular. Why would God make the people of Judah endure seventy years in captivity? Did God truly have their best interests in mind?

The Lord assured the people that they would be blessed generously with a hopeful future if they endured their exile in Babylon. This wasn't the kind of assurance they wanted, but as they faced uncertainty and oppression in a foreign land, the Lord promised that He had plans for His people. Those who submitted to God's timing would be able to call on the Lord and be heard. After years of Israel and Judah's unfaithfulness, this promise was a significant act of mercy on God's part.

Surrender to God's plans is not easy when people believe they know what's best or sup-posed experts suggest alternatives that are more appealing. It's not natural for people to choose seasons of suffering or uncertainty on their own, but God's promise to Israel reminds God's people today that they can expect hope and a future with God if they submit to the more difficult path that God has chosen for to-day. In the end, they may find a prosperity and joy they never could have planned on their own.

PRAYER

Gracious Lord, You form plans that bless Your people and lead them toward safety and peace. Even in times of unfaithfulness, loss, and uncertainty, You stand by Your people and promise to guide them. May we see the wisdom of Your plans and Your direction today as we yield to the path forward You have shown us. Amen.

79. GOD TAKES CARE
OF TOMORROW

*Take therefore no thought for the morrow:
for the morrow shall take thought
for the things of itself.*
MATTHEW 6:34

Jesus was well acquainted with the tendency of His listeners to worry. As He assured them that placing the kingdom of God ahead of every other priority would ensure God's provision and protection, He added that worrying about tomorrow wasn't even worth doing. He encouraged His listeners to focus on what they had to do today rather than wasting time and energy on fears about the next day.

Those who live by faith and trust God to care for them today will see how God can bless them and provide for them despite the worries that may tempt them. They will never see God work through their worries about tomorrow because tomorrow hasn't happened yet! Once the sun rises on a new day, the mercies of God will be fresh again and God will help Christians through their trials and challenges. Setting aside worries about tomorrow frees Christians to focus on the areas of their lives where God can intervene, thereby building their confidence and hope for the future.

Throughout the Bible, the Lord commands His people to remember His past deeds, creating monuments or sharing the stories with future generations, rather than nurturing their fears about tomorrow. By looking back at the Lord's deliverance in the past, they could face the challenges of the present in faith while abandoning worries about the uncertainties of tomorrow. As Christians learn to remain in the present moment with the Lord, they will grow in their confidence and hope.

PRAYER

Father, You have promised Your people that they must seek Your kingdom first and let go of their worries about tomorrow. Remind us of Your past works and help us to surrender our fears and uncertainties to You so that we can remain with You in the present moment, continually turning to You in faith. Amen.

80. GOD OVERCOMES YOUR FEAR

There is no fear in love; but perfect love casteth out fear: because fear hath torment. He that feareth is not made perfect in love.
1 JOHN 4:18

The apostle John wrote with confidence that he knew and believed in God's love for His people. God demonstrated His love by sending Jesus to die as a redemptive sacrifice for sins. In fact, the sacrificial love of Jesus revealed that God is defined by His love. Loving others is a sure way to abide in God, and when God abides in His people, they demonstrate it through loving actions. Those who live in the awareness and experience of God's love have no place in their lives for fear.

Yet for those experiencing fear today, there is no reason for shame. John's letter encourages these Christians to seek God's love and to abide in God. As they grow in the assurance of God's love, they will find a security that pushes fear out of their lives. This security will help them face their worries each day and any concerns they may have about God.

Fear of God's condemnation or of circumstances is a sign that Christians need to be perfected by the present love of God for them. This isn't a one-way grasping for God. God has made the first move, choosing to love people first and making it possible for His people to remain in His love. Learning to live in this love is the great work of believers today. Learning about God's love or hearing about others' experiences with God's love is no substitute for resting in the security of God's love.

PRAYER

Father, You have reached out to Your people in love and compassion, abolishing our fears and anxieties so that we can rest in You and serve others from a place of security. Help us to make space each day to abide in Your love and grow in our awareness of Your loving presence. Amen.

81. GOD GIVES YOU HOPE

Happy is he that hath the God of Jacob for his help, whose hope is in the LORD his God.
PSALM 146:5

The psalmist compares the power of God with the abilities of earthly rulers and authorities. While those who make and enforce the laws of the land or have the political power to control others may believe they hold great power, they have no power compared to God. They cannot even help themselves beyond their few short days. The moment they stop breathing, they are at the mercy of God and have no control. The Lord who made the heavens and the earth holds these powerful rulers in His hand. He can cause them to fall while also caring for His people, bringing peace, justice, and health to the earth. Rather than propping up those in authority, God is most concerned with those suffering injustice or struggling with hunger. He sees those in need and has compassion on them.

God's people today can find hope in the power and presence of the Lord. Rather than serving the changing whims of political power or making compromises to win the favor of those with influence and power, they can rest in the lasting presence of the God who made the world and will continue to sustain it for generations to come. This reliance on God is where joy and peace come from today.

Instead of aligning themselves with leaders whose plans are destined to perish in a short time, God's people are to align themselves with those who are hungry or who need help leaving their troubled past behind. This concern for the most vulnerable also ensures Christians won't place their hope in the powerful rulers who compete with God for influence and power.

PRAYER

Lord, help us to leave our desires for power and influence behind so that we place our trust in You and Your sovereign reign over the earth. May we devote ourselves to the joy of trusting in You and caring for those in need, lest we succumb to the lure of power. Amen.

82. GOD GRANTS PEACE IN TRIBULATIONS

These things I have spoken unto you, that in me ye might have peace. In the world ye shall have tribulation: but be of good cheer; I have overcome the world.
JOHN 16:33

The disciples were on the brink of one of the most terrifying and uncertain periods of their lives as they endured the agony of watching the arrest, trial, and crucifixion of Jesus. They struggled to make sense of what Jesus said about His coming suffering and what it meant for Him to return to the Father. They only knew that the trial coming to Jesus and to them would be so intense that they would abandon Him and go their own ways. Even after all of that, they would still face persecution. Despite all of these dire predictions, Jesus encouraged them to continue to take courage in Him. Although it would appear for a time that the darkness was winning, after His death and resurrection, Jesus would leave them with no doubt that He had indeed conquered the world.

Christians today may not feel like conquerors. They may have great anxiety or concern about the future as they see what looks like one triumph of evil after another. At even the most challenging moments, the followers of Jesus have His assurance that they can trust Him. They will not be abandoned, and their faith in God is not in vain. One day the full power and glory of God will be revealed, ending the charade of principalities and powers.

In Jesus, His people can find peace. Those who struggle to experience His peace or to believe in His victory may be the ones who most urgently need to spend time abiding in Him.

PRAYER

Jesus, You have faced the darkness of our world and conquered it so that You can promise Your people peace and the ultimate victory over evil. Help us to place our complete trust in You and the Father so that we can take courage and remain hopeful in Your victory. Amen.

83. GOD PROMISES YOU A GOOD FUTURE

Being confident of this very thing, that he which hath begun a good work in you will perform it until the day of Jesus Christ.
PHILIPPIANS 1:6

Paul wrote to the Philippian church from his prison cell that he had seen God at work throughout his difficult circumstances, as he watched the church grow in faith and in action and gained many opportunities to share the Gospel. Paul's imprisonment ended up being a way for God to expand Paul's ministry and reveal His faithfulness to complete His good work in Paul. Paul enjoyed the certainty that God would complete His plan for him, whether or not he was in prison. Paul's faith in God's power and purpose rose above his present circumstances, enabling him to believe in God's promise of a good future.

While many Christians today may not relate to the extreme situation of Paul's imprisonment or the persecution faced by the Philippian church, all Christians who share in God's grace and in the message of the Gospel are given the assurance that God will complete His work in them. Those who continue to live in the Gospel message, sharing it with others and praying with joy, can remain in touch with the promise of Paul.

Christians may experience discouraging situations or moments of doubt, but the completion of their faith hinges on the work of Christ. Outside circumstances cannot disrupt the work of Christ in His people who can wait for His return without fear or shame. No outside authority or event can hold off the coming of Christ, undo the work of His cross, or keep God from loving His children.

PRAYER

Jesus, You have graciously made a way to save Your people, and You refuse to allow anything to disrupt Your love for Your people. May we look to You rather than our circumstances for our hope and peace today, trusting that You will accomplish Your purposes in us. Amen.

84. GOD HEARS THE PRAYERS OF THE HUMBLE

LORD, thou hast heard the desire of the humble:
thou wilt prepare their heart, thou wilt cause
thine ear to hear.
PSALM 10:17

In the days when the psalms were being written, many idols and kings were attempting to compete with the Lord for devotion, influence, and worship. The Lord is a jealous God who shows great mercy and compassion to His people but refuses to share His glory or power with any imposter. The psalmist prayed that those who opposed God and His people would be exposed and then broken. While God opposes those who attack others or seek to build their own wealth and power at any cost, those who are meek and humble are promised that God will hear them.

Humility is often praised as an essential aspect of prayer because it ensures that those seeking the Lord recognize their place before God, have an appropriate awe of the Lord and His power, and aren't trying to use God's favor for their own gain. In contrast to the wicked and evildoers who exploit widows and orphans and those struggling economically, God's people recognize that their well-being rests in God's mercy and blessings, so they take up the Lord's cause of justice. When praying with humility, God's people recognize that they are only capable of acting within the calling of the Lord. As they humble themselves before the Lord, they will receive the strength they need to carry out God's plans in the world. In the end, God's purposes will be fulfilled and justice will be carried out, while evildoers will be removed from the earth.

PRAYER

Lord, You are all-powerful and strong, able to carry out Your will and to overcome the plans of the wicked in our world. May we humbly take our place before You and trust in Your power to strengthen us to serve others. May we value justice and peace for those who are suffering, lest we lose sight of the grace and blessings You give to us. Amen.

PROMISES OF HEALING

85. GOD GIVES YOU HEALING

He healeth the broken in heart,
and bindeth up their wounds.
PSALM 147:3

As the people of Israel looked to rebuild their nation after the exile, they had no other hope than the power and grace of God. They had been scattered throughout a foreign country and returned to a ruined and vulnerable country. As they pondered their future, they sang songs of praise and remembered the graciousness of God, trusting that the Lord would help them gather together again and rebuild their nation. The outcasts of Israel would see God at work among them, healing their broken hearts and treating their wounds. Reflecting on God's creative powers in the world reassured them that the God who set the stars in their places was more than able to restore their lives.

Those who seek God today, whether from a position of brokenness or a season of exile, can count on God's grace and restoration. God's power extends to His wounded people and makes their healing possible, bringing ruins back to life and restoring what has been broken. God never desires to see His people suffer or endure a season of painful loss, but He does take joy in healing His people and reestablishing them. Many who have experienced God's healing and restoration have even found that their pain became a source for their ministry as well, allowing them to share the healing of God with others who have suffered similar wounds and losses. Just as God brought the world into being out of chaos, He is capable of bringing peace and hope out of situations of loss and discouragement.

PRAYER

Father, You desire to bring healing to those who are wounded and hurt, restoring the lives of those who appear hopeless and damaged. May we experience the mercy of this creative work and show Your love to those who seek You. Amen.

86. GOD GIVES YOU POWER
TO HEAL OTHERS

*To another faith by the same Spirit; to another
the gifts of healing by the same Spirit. . .*
1 CORINTHIANS 12:9

The Corinthian church ministered to many through the gifts of the Spirit that God gave them in spite of their moral struggles and failures. However, each of the Corinthian believers had different gifts and roles to play in the wider body of Christ. Some may have envied the ability of some to believe in God with great confidence, while others could have viewed the gift of healing as a kind of superior gift. Paul assured them that their spiritual gifts were assigned by the Holy Spirit who united them together in the one body of Christ. They all participated in these gifts through the Holy Spirit and could not take any personal credit for their special abilities.

Christians today can benefit from trusting in the Holy Spirit to empower them for ministry and to unite them with the wider church. There may be situations where a Christian with the gift of healing can help those who are suffering, while on other occasions a Christian struggling with unbelief may need the support offered through the prayers of those with a particularly strong faith. The differences in the church become a strength when each member looks to their empowerment by the Spirit and trusts that God can make them effective through His power and direction. There is no hierarchy when all are united in God through the indwelling Spirit.

PRAYER

Jesus, You have granted us Your Holy Spirit to empower us to serve others and minister healing to all in need. May we take our place in Your company of believers by trusting the Spirit to help us serve effectively, giving You the glory and honoring those who help build up the body of Christ.

87. GOD GIVES YOU GOOD SLEEP

*When thou liest down, thou shalt
not be afraid: yea, thou shalt lie
down, and thy sleep shall be sweet.*
PROVERBS 3:24

The sayings of the Proverbs encouraged the people of Israel to place their trust in the Lord and the wisdom He grants to His people. By relying on the Lord's wisdom and direction, they could be certain to avoid grievous mistakes, steer clear of sudden panic, and live in a state of security and peace. Those who placed their hope in the Lord's wisdom were promised confidence and peace that would extend even to their slumber.

God's wisdom is still being offered to His people today. He promises rest to those who place their confidence in His direction. Abandoning the teachings of scripture and neglecting the gift of the Spirit will result in a season of stumbling, uncertainty, and even fear. A sleepless night may even be in the future of those who choose their own wisdom and desires over the wisdom of God.

When a tragedy strikes or a season of difficulty comes, God's people can get a sense of where they've placed their hope by examining their response. Are they able to meet their challenges with the quiet confidence of God's wisdom, or are they thrown into panic and chaos? By regularly keeping the wisdom of God before themselves each day, they will develop an awareness of and confidence in God's guidance. The process may be gradual, with the fruit showing up over time. However, the rest and peace that come from seeking the Lord will grow and multiply over time.

PRAYER

Lord, You offer peace and rest to Your people today, leading them toward the way of wisdom and offering guidance for their decisions. May we place our confidence in You and rest each day in the power and strength You give to those who place their faith in You. Amen.

88. GOD GIVES YOU REST AND RECUPERATION

*Come unto me, all ye that labour and
are heavy laden, and I will give you rest.*
MATTHEW 11:28

Jesus was surrounded by religious leaders who worked hard to obey the law of God and to preserve their traditions. He described their rules and efforts as heavy burdens that they often bore publicly in order to win the respect and approval of the people who looked up to them. However, the laws they eagerly bore as part of their "careers" as religious leaders were often too difficult for the average person to bear. At times the people struggled to keep the Sabbath when the safety of their animals was at stake; other times they had difficulty determining how much to tithe from their gardens as religious leaders debated the demands of the law. As a result, the people often felt burdened by the law of God rather than freed by it.

Jesus promised a different approach to God that fulfilled the law without being overwhelmed by it. He spoke of His easy yoke that He would share with His disciples as they learned from Him and joined Him in bearing His light burden, all the while abiding in God's transforming love and presence. The heavy burdens of the law teachers would not weigh them down.

Disciples of Jesus today receive the same invitation to lay down their heavy burdens and find refreshment from their weariness by following Jesus. His gentleness and humility will not cause stress or strain but will lead people toward rest for their souls. What He asks of them is easy to bear and will not leave them weary. Rather, they will be invigorated and encouraged to move forward, obeying His commands without getting lost in overwhelming man-made restrictions.

PRAYER

Jesus, You promise peace and restoration for Your people, rather than the praise and accolades that the religious experts seek. May we take up Your yoke and carry Your burden alongside You so that we may live as Your faithful people while finding rest for our souls. Amen.

89. GOD HELPS YOU
BREAK BAD HABITS

*I can do all things through Christ
which strengtheneth me.*
PHILIPPIANS 4:13

While sitting alone in a prison cell, Paul took comfort in the strength of Christ and looked to Christ to help him endure his days in prison. But his dependence on Christ wasn't something he learned to put into practice while in jail. Rather, his faith in God's deliverance was cultivated over time as he faced one trial after another. Whether facing financial hardship, isolation, hunger, criticism, or the heavy hand of Roman authorities, Paul learned to remain content in the power of God at work in his life. Even when it appeared all of his resources had dried up and he had nowhere left to turn, the Lord stood by him and offered him His matchless comfort.

Paul shows Christians today that true contentment is not measured by material markers. There is no financial target for blessing or contentment under God. The secret of being content is relying on God's unfailing love for His people. When God is the source of confidence for Christians, they will find the strength and ability to do whatever God has called them to accomplish. While every Christian would rightly pray for God to provide food in a time of hunger or liberty in a time of oppression, improved circumstances will not lead to contentment.

Consumer society has proven that people can never be fully content with food and possessions since there's always one more thing to try or buy. In Christ, Christians find that they have access to God's abundant blessings to face their challenges each day.

PRAYER

Jesus, You stand by Your people in times of plenty and in times of need, empowering them to bear up under heavy burdens and to stand strong in times of uncertainty. Give us confidence in Your power and presence today as we trust You to provide for our needs. Amen.

90. GOD GIVES YOU
VICTORY OVER ANGER

*He that is slow to anger is better than
the mighty; and he that ruleth his
spirit than he that taketh a city.*
PROVERBS 16:32

The book of Proverbs portrays anger as a liability for the people of Israel because it easily becomes fixated on personal demands and even one's sense of pride and accomplishment. If left unchecked, anger creates division and damages important relationships. It wasn't too much to say that anger allowed free rein could unravel God's work in His people and leave them fragmented and prideful. Anger was seen as a fatal flaw for kings and rulers especially, as it undermined any influence or accomplishments they could claim to their names.

Ruling one's spirit, preventing anger from taking over, was viewed on the scale of conquering a city. Of course, taking control of a city required significant planning, resources, and patience. Leaders who succeeded in such a campaign had to invest significantly in the endeavor, and Proverbs suggests that overcoming anger is just as demanding.

By turning over their anger and their demands to God, the people of God today can live by faith, trusting that God will avenge their enemies and give them justice. Those who live seeking praise or power from men will certainly fall into the trap of anger sooner rather than later. However, those who trust God with their future will be able to meet the unexpected parts of their days and even their failures with a sense of perspective and peace. Knowing that God is able to work through the hardships as well as the positive outcomes, God's people can find deliverance from anger and the peace of Christ that passes all understanding.

PRAYER

Lord, You save Your people from their sins and the lure of anger. May we see ourselves as Your humble children in need of Your mercy and live by faith that You can defend us and lead us. May we conduct our lives with grace and kindness toward others as we experience the love You show to us. Amen.

91. GOD GIVES YOU
VICTORY OVER ANXIETIES

Search me, O God, and know my heart:
try me, and know my thoughts.
PSALM 139:23

With particularly stark language, Psalm 139 addresses the seriousness of disobedience and the urgency of rejecting actions that counter the teachings of the Lord. The psalmist expresses his strong hatred of anyone who is opposed to the Lord, which may be traced back to the history of Israel's exiles and military defeats that were precipitated by abandoning the Lord, ignoring His laws, and perpetuating injustice throughout the land. The stakes were extremely high for the people of Israel, and this perception of disobedience leading to national calamity could be one of the reasons this psalm adopts such a vigilant approach to sin, asking God to search the hearts of His people in order to test them and either prove they are pure or expose and correct any errors.

Today's psalm is a good prayer to use at the close of each day, inviting God to reveal any hidden sins, destructive patterns of thinking, or subtle shifts away from God's redemption and love. The Psalms make it clear that God already knows what His people are thinking, so God's people would be wise to cooperatively open themselves up to the Spirit's scrutiny on a daily basis. As the Spirit brings up sins, moral failures, or misconceptions, God's people have an opportunity to repent and ask for God's guidance in the ways of everlasting life.

Forgoing this kind of spiritual scrutiny is a dangerous risk that could lead God's people to drift away from His path and ignore His presence in their lives. Failure to confess their sins could lead to hardened hearts that become increasingly resistant to the Lord's direction.

PRAYER

Father, You know the hearts of Your people and will guide them in the way of everlasting life if they will submit to Your gentle guidance. May we see the destructive power of our sins and acts of disobedience so that we can turn to You and enjoy the peace of being reoriented by Your Spirit. Amen.

PROMISES OF ETERNAL LIFE

92. GOD PROMISES YOU ETERNAL LIFE

And this is life eternal, that they might know thee the only true God, and Jesus Christ, whom thou hast sent.
JOHN 17:3

Jesus had the single goal of revealing God to humanity, making it possible for all people to experience eternal life in union with God. This "eternal" life extends forever, but according to Jesus, it also begins in the present for anyone who knows God the Father and Jesus the Son. The Father gave all authority to the Son so that He could grant this new redemptive life in God to as many people as possible. Even in the final moments of Jesus' ministry, He prayed with thankfulness and joy that He was able to reveal the Father and bring Him glory throughout the earth. In His final moments, Jesus prayed that the Father would be glorified through His sacrifice and that all of His completed work would continue to draw attention to the Father.

While Jesus understandably could have focused on His own life and impending death, He chose instead to pray for His followers, asking that they would know God the Father better. He sought to ensure they would have access to God's eternal life and experience the peace that He passed on to them.

The mission of Jesus hinged on His self-sacrifice and willingness to glorify God the Father, making Him known to as many people as possible. Christians today have a similar mission: live sacrificially, reveal God to as many people as possible, and draw all the glory to God. The Spirit remains with Jesus' people to guide them, to direct their words, and to help them let go of sinful desires in order to bring glory to God.

PRAYER

Jesus, You grant Your people eternal life and unite them with the love of the Father so that they can enter Your rest. Give us a spirit of humility and self-sacrifice as we tell others about Your love and salvation today, and may we win You the honor and glory with our lives. Amen.

93. GOD PROMISES
TO COMFORT YOU

Yea, though I walk through the valley of the shadow of death, I will fear no evil: for thou art with me; thy rod and thy staff they comfort me.
PSALM 23:4

God does not abandon His people in the midst of hard times, but He also doesn't spare them from all hardship and difficulty. This psalm of David shares that evil may be lurking for God's people and dark times can be expected, but God remains by His people to provide protection and comfort. The people of Israel knew all too well about facing danger repeatedly, but the covenant of God, His love for His people, and His presence with them were never in doubt.

David himself underwent some intense journeys in the valley of the shadow of death, where calamity awaited him at every turn. However, the Lord delivered him and reaffirmed His promise to remain faithful for generations. Even when the circumstances of life appear dark or hopeless, God's people can always rely on the Lord's presence.

While struggles are guaranteed, God's people must decide today whom they will look to as their shepherd. The Bible includes story after story of God's people choosing to follow false shepherds and blind guides who told them what they wanted to hear. However, when difficulty struck, these false shepherds either fled or switched sides for their own benefit. The Lord is faithful and trustworthy, protecting those entrusted to His care. Under the Lord's care, His people will find comfort, contentment, provision, and rest, even when the circumstances of life are difficult.

PRAYER

Jesus, You called Yourself the Good Shepherd because You seek out the lost sheep, guard them sacrificially with Your own life, and make sure that they lie down in safety and security. May our souls find rest and safety in Your care, and may we live with the contentment that comes through Your guidance. Amen.

94. GOD PROMISES YOU GLORY

*In God is my salvation and my glory: the rock
of my strength, and my refuge, is in God.*
PSALM 62:7

Looking to the Lord as their refuge and waiting in silence for His salvation prompt God's people to stop relying on their own ideas, connections, and resources. When God's people resolve to wait for the Lord to guide their steps and look to Him as a fortress of protection, they will find God's glory and deliverance when He finally acts. This posture of dependence and expectation is not an easy choice. There may be many urgent matters to address and plenty of people offering opinions and counsel on how best to move forward. The longer God's people have to wait, the greater the chance a crisis will ensue.

When God's people take the initiative and act on their own, they lose an opportunity to experience God's intervention and to win God the glory. Today many Christians are surrounded by news cycles, advice experts, self-help books, and volatile markets that all urge action and change. Who has time to wait for God's direction? In addition, what is there to do while waiting for God? This psalm suggests that God's people will wait for Him in silence.

While the waiting may not be pleasant, God's reward for His people will be. God shares His salvation and deliverance with those who look to Him. They will have stories to tell future generations of God's love and concern, while also bolstering their own faith for the next crisis that arises. They will find that trusting in God throughout the years will build a sturdy foundation, a rock that will weather the threats of any storm.

PRAYER

Lord, You have promised to be a rock,
a fortress, and a sure foundation for those
who wait on Your help and depend on You.
Give us patience to wait and softened hearts
that are willing to obey Your commands.
May our faith grow as we experience Your
deliverance and provision this week. Amen.

95. GOD PROMISES REWARDS FOR FAITHFULNESS

Blessed is the man that endureth temptation: for when he is tried, he shall receive the crown of life, which the Lord hath promised to them that love him.
JAMES 1:12

In the heat of the moment, Christians may find it difficult to resist temptation. It may even appear irresistible. James wrote to a group of Christians who had many struggles and sins to work through, from remaining pure to taming their tongues to judging one another based on appearance. All of these temptations added up for the beleaguered church, and it's likely that many of the Christians reading his letter were discouraged or even on the brink of giving up. Could they endure all of these temptations and trials?

James expands the vision of his readers into the larger picture of sin, temptation, and holiness. Enduring and overcoming temptation will pay off in the future when God rewards His people for their faithfulness. As God tests the actions (and inaction) of His servants, He will reward those who endure with the crown of life. Those who choose to live in obedience to God in this life will be rewarded for their choices in the next.

Moreover, of particular interest to readers facing temptation today, James offers a clue about how the church can resist the temptations they face. God will reward those who love Him. Loving God is a kind of indirect way to counteract sin and temptation. By focusing on the goodness of the Lord and His generous gift of life for His people, they can grow in their love and commitment. This commitment, which is rooted and grounded in love, will help them remain in Him rather than entertaining the possibility of disobedience. In the end, those who are spurred to obey God out of love will reap the rewards He promises.

PRAYER

Father, You love Your people and offer them the reward of life for their faithfulness today. May we respond to Your overtures of love and choose to live our lives according to Your will, resisting the pull of temptation and entering into the life You have promised to us. Amen.

96. GOD PROMISES REWARDS FOR GOOD DEEDS

O love the L ORD, all ye his saints:
for the L ORD preserveth the faithful,
and plentifully rewardeth the proud doer.
P SALM 31:23

Many of the psalms were written in response to dangerous situations, extreme alarms, and significant tests of faith. From military sieges to intrigue and deception among enemies, the psalmists wanted their readers to know that the Lord would stand by His people and preserve them in the face of affliction, attack, or conspiracy. The only recourse for God's people is to call out to the Lord in faith, sharing the full extent of their concerns. The Lord will hear His people because of His great love for them and because of their faithfulness to His commands.

However, those who forget the Lord and seek to advance themselves will find that God is silent in their hour of need. Pride is what precedes a fall, and it blocks people from depending on the Lord. Those who love the Lord will see His faithfulness in response to their dependence on Him, but the prideful will reap the consequences of their self-reliance and self-preservation.

While God hears the prayers of His people today, they may have to wait for an answer, and they may not get the answer they are expecting. Nonetheless, those who live in faithful obedience, loving the Lord because of His mercy and grace, can expect that God will respond to their requests and preserve them in their time of trial. Obedience is not overlooked or taken for granted because it is the sign of a loving commitment to the Lord, and the Lord always remains faithful to His people.

PRAYER

Lord, You take great delight in preserving Your faithful people and guiding them to a place of peace and security. May we turn to You with our requests in faith and hope, waiting on You with patience and courage to deliver us from the trouble that awaits us today. Amen.

97. GOD PROMISES YOU AN ETERNAL DWELLING

In my Father's house are many mansions:
if it were not so, I would have told you.
I go to prepare a place for you.
JOHN 14:2

There was no escaping the loss and sorrow that awaited the disciples as they learned about the coming death and departure of Jesus. Their time with Him was short. Although they would soon experience His presence through the Holy Spirit, they would miss the security of spending their days and evenings with Him. In this time of uncertainty and sadness, Jesus offered a word of encouragement for His disciples: they would one day dwell with Him in His Father's house. Because of their faithfulness to the Father, they would enter into God's rest and dwell forever in the place Jesus prepared for them.

For those who believe that Jesus is the way, the truth, and the life today, Jesus also assures them that they can join Him in His dwelling place with God the Father. It's true that Christians today know very little about where Jesus is going or even how to get there, but they do know the One who will come to take them to His dwelling place.

Of course, many will doubt the words of Jesus today, and His disciples were no different. Jesus assures those who doubt or remain uneasy that their hearts should not be troubled about the future. He would never tell them such a fantastic thing if it wasn't true. God's people have His guarantee that they will join Him in the peace and security of His heavenly home. Even today, Jesus is waiting for His people. The rooms have been prepared and they can find peace and comfort knowing that the next step of their journey has already been set for them.

PRAYER

Jesus, You care for those who follow You and have graciously offered assurance of eternal peace in Your company in Your Father's house. May we find comfort and confidence in this promise as we share the good news of Your love with others. Amen.

98. GOD PROMISES REUNIONS
WITH LOVED ONES

Thy dead men shall live, together with my dead
body shall they arise. Awake and sing, ye that
dwell in dust: for thy dew is as the dew of herbs,
and the earth shall cast out the dead.
ISAIAH 26:19

The Lord brings restoration and life to people who have suffered and lost seemingly everything. The people of Israel who had seemingly vanished from the earth during the exile were like dead corpses scattered on the dust of the earth. How could they ever come alive to sing God's praises again? What hope did they have after losing so much and watching their hopes and plans fall to pieces?

While men could hardly imagine a way to restore those who had fallen, God made a promise of resurrection that appeared too good to be true. Just as dew falls on the earth, God's mercy would settle on those who had departed and raise them up. This restoration was a complete and total gift from God, given out of His love for His people and His desire to see them rise up to sing for joy again.

The hope of the resurrection that Christians hold to today has roots that stretch back to the prophets. The people of Israel also looked to the hope of resurrection one day, and Jesus came as God's guarantee to make good on His promise, becoming the first of many to rise from the dead to new life. In times of death, hopelessness, or discouragement, God's people can look to the resurrection of Jesus as a reminder that God can bring the dead back to life. There may be a season of loss and devastation, but in the end, God conquers even the darkness of death, restoring His people to one another on the other side of this life.

PRAYER

Jesus, You have conquered death and risen to new life just as the prophets promised long ago. May we take comfort in the promise of new life and live by faith in Your decisive defeat of death as we wait to be reunited with those who have passed before us. Amen.

99. GOD SPARES YOU FROM JUDGMENT

The Lord knoweth how to deliver the godly out of temptations, and to reserve the unjust unto the day of judgment to be punished.
2 PETER 2:9

Peter wrote to a church that was suffering both persecution from authorities and division from false prophets. While it appeared they were being attacked on all sides with no end in sight, Peter reminded them that God was well aware of their situation and would one day take action in a number of ways. While judgment awaited those who embraced false teaching, sin, and division in the church, there was also the assurance that God would preserve His people and keep them from judgment. Peter even goes through a lengthy lesson in the history of God's people before making his point. Just as the Lord saved Noah and Lot from the judgment of their time, the Lord would rescue His people from the extreme persecution and ungodliness around them.

The church today may be discouraged, especially in parts of the world where oppressive regimes limit the freedom of worship. Even in countries with significant freedom, however, there can be division and conflict causing Christians to despair. They may wonder, *Does God notice what is going on here? Will the righteous be recognized for their faithfulness?* Peter's letter reminds Christians that God knows who is faithful and who is indulging in their own desires. One day the Lord will call these people to account for their actions, while justifying those who quietly pursued Him and His kingdom. That day may not come soon enough for many Christians, but Peter's long list of God's past judgments and rescues drives home the point that God will one day follow through on His promises.

PRAYER

Sovereign Lord, You see our sins and our good deeds. You know our hearts completely. May we live each day aware of Your promise to rescue Your people from judgment and to recognize the good we have done, even if no one ever sees the ways we have remained faithful. Amen.

100. GOD PROMISES AUTHORITY OVER NATIONS

And he that overcometh, and keepeth
my works unto the end, to him will
I give power over the nations.
REVELATION 2:26

As John shared the Lord's revelation to the churches throughout modern-day Turkey, he sought to encourage them as they suffered persecution from the local authorities. Within the church itself, however, an even greater threat was being tolerated and claiming the faith of many Christians. A false teacher had been distorting the Gospel, but Jesus promised He would come to expose this false teaching and hold its adherents accountable. The rest of the church that rejected this teaching and held fast to what they had been given were promised a very different fate. After a period of suffering both in the public sphere and within their churches, they would one day be recognized as conquerors and even placed in positions of authority over nations as Jesus took His rightful place as King of kings and Lord of lords on earth.

Such an unlikely promise to a small, humble

church suffering persecution drives home the power of Jesus for Christians today who may be tempted to seek earthly positions of power and influence. While it may seem appealing to work toward gaining positions that are recognized by earthly authorities, the promise of Jesus is a helpful antidote. The kingdom of God may advance in small mustard seeds and among the people who are counted as insignificant by most people in the world or even in the church, but in God's kingdom those who are humble and faithful are the most likely to be rewarded with positions of authority and power.

PRAYER

Jesus, You promise to save Your people and to bless them richly in the age to come. May we hold on to the faith that has been passed on to us and reject the lure of power or false teachings that could keep us from You. May we find peace and comfort in Your kingdom one day. Amen.

101. GOD BLESSES
FAITHFUL BELIEVERS

Blessed is he that readeth, and they that hear the words of this prophecy, and keep those things which are written therein: for the time is at hand.
REVELATION 1:3

The churches in Asia Minor were given a message about both the trials they were facing and the power of God that would be manifested one day on earth. This message would prove critical for their faithfulness. If they had any hope of holding on to the teachings of Christ and believing in the Gospel message, they would need to hear and put the words of this prophecy into practice. Much like the wise man who built his life on the solid foundation of Jesus' words and committed himself to the hard but rewarding work of obedience, the churches were promised blessings from God if they kept the words that John passed on to them.

Christians can expect plenty of challenges, disappointments, and sorrows in this world, and the churches that endured some of the worst persecution and uncertainty offer a helpful model of how Jesus expects His people to persevere. In a sense, Christians can look at the teachings of scripture as a kind of lifeline that will pull them out of the confusion and distractions of today's culture. Through learning and practicing the words of scripture, they will be prepared for spiritual attacks, opposition from those outside the faith, and even misdirection from those who have distorted the faith. By basing their choices on the words of Jesus, they will be assured of God's blessing and a place in His kingdom when He returns to rule the earth in peace and justice at the end of this age.

PRAYER

Jesus, You promise to bless those who keep Your teachings and live in obedience to Your commands. May we turn away from every competing philosophy, mode of thinking, and priority in our lives so that we can look to You and the wisdom of Your Word. Amen.

ABOUT THE AUTHOR

Ed Cyzewski is the author of *Flee, Be Silent, Pray* as well as *A Christian Survival Guide: A Lifeline to Faith and Growth* and *Coffee-house Theology: Reflecting on God in Everyday Life* and is the co-author of *The Good News of Revelation* and *Unfollowers: Unlikely Lessons on Faith from Those Who Doubted Jesus.* He writes about prayer and imperfectly following Jesus at www.edcyzewski.com.